Green Finance and Investment

Access to Green Finance for SMEs in Georgia

This work is published under the responsibility of the Secretary-General of the OECD. The opinions expressed and arguments employed herein do not necessarily reflect the official views of OECD member countries.

This document, as well as any data and map included herein, are without prejudice to the status of or sovereignty over any territory, to the delimitation of international frontiers and boundaries and to the name of any territory, city or area.

The statistical data for Israel are supplied by and under the responsibility of the relevant Israeli authorities. The use of such data by the OECD is without prejudice to the status of the Golan Heights, East Jerusalem and Israeli settlements in the West Bank under the terms of international law.

Please cite this publication as:
OECD (2019), *Access to Green Finance for SMEs in Georgia*, Green Finance and Investment, OECD Publishing, Paris, *https://doi.org/10.1787/dc98f97b-en*.

ISBN 978-92-64-44541-3 (print)
ISBN 978-92-64-95861-6 (pdf)

Green Finance and Investment
ISSN 2409-0336 (print)
ISSN 2409-0344 (online)

Photo credits: Cover © mika48/Shutterstock.com.

Corrigenda to publications may be found on line at: *www.oecd.org/about/publishing/corrigenda.htm*.
© OECD 2019

The use of this work, whether digital or print, is governed by the Terms and Conditions to be found at *http://www.oecd.org/termsandconditions*.

Foreword

Small and medium-sized enterprises (SMEs) play an important role in Georgia's economy. SMEs provide more than 67% of employment and 61.5% of gross value added. Although the environmental footprint of individual SMEs may be low, their aggregate impact in many respects exceeds that of large businesses. SMEs have a particularly significant environmental impact in such sectors as food processing, minerals extraction and tourism (hotels and restaurants).

Commercial banks play an important role in providing access to green finance, including for SMEs. However, market conditions in the European Union Eastern Partnership (EaP) countries constrain the involvement of commercial banks. Generally, they have only established specific environmental credit lines when supported by international financial institutions (IFIs). Only a small number continue to offer such products once IFI support is withdrawn. Learning from the design and implementation of such credit lines can provide useful insights into how to increase the capacity and willingness of the banking sector to finance green investments to SMEs.

This report reviews the experience of developing environmental credit lines in Georgia and using them to lend to SMEs. It reviews the macroeconomic and political context for green investments in the country. It then analyses in more detail the role and capacity of the banking sector and the policy environment for green investment and broader access to finance for SMEs. Further, the report examines the experience of three banks in Georgia (Bank of Georgia, TBC Bank and ProCredit Bank). Specifically, it assesses barriers to developing a successfully sustainable energy-lending portfolio and to identifying key success factors from the institutional perspective. These banks are well-positioned to take part in this analysis as they are the largest local financial institutions that benefit from IFI-supported environmental credit lines in Georgia.

The report was drafted by Matthew Savage (Oxford Consulting Partners) with inputs by Nelly Petkova (OECD Environment), who also led and managed overall project implementation. The report was reviewed by Krzysztof Michalak, David Simek and Takayoshi Kato (OECD Environment Directorate) and their suggestions are very much appreciated. Many colleagues from Georgia contributed to this analysis and special thanks go to: Davit Advadze and Tsisnami Sabadze (Ministry of Economy and Sustainable Development [MESD]), Ani Vashakmadze (Georgia's Innovation and Technology Agency), Tamara Khizanishvili and Keti Bitskinashvili (TBC Bank), Ketevan Mumladze and Natia Kalandarishvili (Bank of Georgia), Ketevan Kekelashvili (ProCredit Bank), Andreas Berkhof (European Investment Bank), Tatiana Chernyavskaya (United Nations Industrial Development Organization), Mikheil Khuchua (GIZ Georgia), Malkhaz Adeishvili (United Nations Development Programme Georgia), Giorgi Mukhigulishvili (World Experience for Georgia). Participants at the National Policy Dialogue meeting, which was held as part of this work on 16 July 2019 in Tbilisi, discussed major findings. This debate helped us further improve the analysis. The project team is in debt to Deputy Minister of Economy and Sustainable Development Ekaterine Mikabadze and Irma

Kavtaradze (former Deputy Minister of MESD) for their support, advice and engagement during project implementation.

Aleksandra Bogusz and Maria Dubois provided overall administrative support for the project. Soojin Jeong helped prepare the meeting in Tbilisi and her involvement was indispensable. Peter Carlson and Lupita Johanson provided valuable communication support around the project. Mark Foss edited the text.

The completion of this work would not have been possible without the support of all these colleagues and their contributions are gratefully acknowledged.

This study forms part of a larger OECD project examining the conditions that would enable commercial banks in the EaP countries to support green investments.

The study was implemented within the framework and with the financial support of the "Greening Economies in the European Union's Eastern Neighbourhood" (EaP GREEN) project and the "EU for Environment" project. These aim to support the six EaP countries (Armenia, Azerbaijan, Belarus, Georgia, Republic of Moldova and Ukraine) to move towards a green economy by decoupling economic growth from environmental degradation and resource depletion. This study was also supported by the German Federal Ministry for the Environment, Nature Conservation and Nuclear Safety through its International Climate Initiative.

The views expressed in this report are those of the authors and do not necessarily reflect those of the European Union, the OECD or their respective member countries.

Table of Contents

Foreword 3

Abbreviations and acronyms 9

Executive summary 11

Chapter 1. The macroeconomic context for green investments in Georgia 15
    1.1. Political context 16
    1.2. Macroeconomic situation 16
    1.3. Macroeconomic situation 18
    1.4. Forward outlook 20
    Notes 20
    References 21

Chapter 2. Small and medium-sized enterprise policy in Georgia 23
    2.1. Context for SME development 24
    2.2. Definitions of SMEs in Georgia 24
    2.3. SME policy environment 25
    2.4. National SME development strategy 26
    2.5. Institutional support 27
    2.6. Programmes and measures to support SMEs 28
    2.7. Emerging measures 28
    2.8. Barriers to access to finance 28
    2.9. Financing structures 30
    2.10. Market gap for green SME investments 31
    References 32

Chapter 3. Energy, Environmental and Climate Policy of Georgia 35
    3.1. Context 36
    3.2. Renewable energy 39
    3.3. Potential areas for strengthening 39
    Notes 40
    References 41

Chapter 4. Climate finance for SMEs in Georgia 43
    4.1. Overview 44
    4.2. Georgian credit market 44
    4.3. Green credit 46
    4.4. Local banks that provide green finance in Georgia 48
    4.5. Key success factors 49
    4.6. Key challenges 50
    4.7. Policy response 53
    Notes 55
    References 56

Chapter 5. Recommendations for policy makers 57
    5.1. Strengthen environmental policy and regulation 58
    5.2. Define role of SMEs in the green transition 60
    5.3. Improve wider access to finance for SMEs 60
    5.4. Improve the availability and terms of green finance for SMEs 62
    5.5. Scale the overall availability of green finance in the Georgian economy 63
    5.6. Raise awareness among SMEs of green transition opportunities 64
    References 65

Annex A. Georgia's banking sector 67
    Market structure and concentration 67
    Trends in the banking sector 68
    Ongoing reform 71
    References 72

Annex B. SME low-cost energy and resource efficiency investments 73

Tables

Table 2.1. New Georgian definitions of SMEs 25
Table 2.2. EU definition of SMEs 25
Table 3.1. Overview of relevant energy and environmental policy development in Georgia 37
Table 4.1. Overview of Georgia's financial institutions receiving IFI support 48

Table A A.1. Consolidation in the Georgian banking market 68

Figures

Figure 1.1. Real GDP growth rates 2008-18, annual percentage 17
Figure 1.2. GEL: USD Exchange rate, 2008-18 17
Figure 1.3. Georgia annual consumer inflation, 2008-18, percentage 18
Figure 1.4. Georgia key monetary policy interest rate, 2008-18, percentage per annum 18
Figure 1.5. Georgia country ranking: "Doing Business" report 2008-18 19
Figure 1.6. Gross fixed capital formation, share of GDP, 2008-18 19
Figure 1.7. Foreign direct investment net inflows as a share of GDP, 2008-18 20
Figure 4.1. Growth in credit vs GDP growth in Georgian banks, share per annum, 2012-18 45

Figure A A.1. Non-banking financial assets as a share of total assets, 2008-18 67
Figure A A.2. Regulatory capital adequacy ratio for Georgian banks (Basel III), percentage, 2014-18 69
Figure A A.3. Non-performing loans for Georgian banks, share, 2008-18 69
Figure A A.4. Return on equity of Georgian Banks, 2008-18, share 70
Figure A A.5. Georgian banks customer deposits to overall loans, share, 2008-18 70
Figure A A.6. Share of foreign currency-denominated loans issued by Georgian banks, 2008-18 71

Boxes

Box 4.1. IFIs involved in green financing in Georgia 46
Box 4.2. Examples of criteria for ProCredit Bank eco loans 53

Abbreviations and acronyms

AA	Association Agreement
APMA	Agricultural Projects Management Agency
BAU	Business as usual
BoG	Bank of Georgia
CAR	Capital adequacy ratio
CGS	Credit guarantee scheme
COP	Conference of the Parties under the UNFCCC
DCFTA	Deep and Comprehensive Free Trade Area
EaP	EU Eastern Partnership
EaP GREEN	EU-supported "Greening Economies in the European Union's Eastern Neighbourhood" Project
EBRD	European Bank for Reconstruction and Development
EC	European Commission
EDA/Enterprise Georgia	Georgian Enterprise Development Agency
EE	Energy efficiency
EIB	European Investment Bank
EU	European Union
FC	Foreign currency
FDI	Foreign direct investment
FI	(Local) financing institution
FTSE	Financial Times and Stock Exchange (index)
GCCI	Georgian Chamber of Commerce and Industry
GCPF	Global Climate Partnership Fund
GDP	Gross domestic product
GEL	Georgian Lari (national currency)
GGF	Green for Growth Fund
GHG	Greenhouse gas
GITA	Georgia's Innovation and Technology Agency
GIZ	Deutsche Gesellschaft für Internationale Zusammenarbeit (German Development Co-operation)

GoG	Government of Georgia
IFC	International Finance Corporation
IFI	International financial institution
KfW	Kreditanstalt für Wiederaufbau, German government-owned development bank
LEDS	Low-emission development strategy
LULUCF	Land use, land-use change and forestry
MESD	Ministry of Economy and Sustainable Development
MFOs	Microfinance organisations
NAMA	Nationally Appropriate Mitigation Action
NAP	National Adaptation Plan
NATO	North Atlantic Treaty Organization
NBG	National Bank of Georgia
NDC	Nationally Determined Contribution
NEEAP	National Energy Efficiency Action Plan
NPL	Non-performing loan
OECD	Organisation for Economic Co-operation and Development
OeEB	Development Bank of Austria
RE	Renewable energy
RIA	Regulatory Impact Assessment
RoE	Return on equity
SBA	Small Business Act for Europe
SEAP	Sustainable Energy Action Plans
SHP	Small hydropower
SME	Small and medium-sized enterprise
UNDP	United Nations Development Programme
UNFCCC	United Nations Framework Convention on Climate Change
UNIDO	United Nations Industrial Development Organization
VAT	Value added tax

Measure units

CO_2	Carbon dioxide
$MtCO_2e$	Million tonnes of carbon dioxide equivalent
MW	Megawatt
MWh	Megawatt hour
tCO_2	Tonne of carbon dioxide

Executive summary

SME policy environment

The Georgian economy relies heavily on small and medium-sized enterprises (SMEs), which provide more than 67% of employment and 61.5% of gross value added. Georgia performs strongly under the OECD SME Policy Index as the best performing country in the EU Eastern Partnership (EaP) region, with robust SME development policies and frameworks. However, SMEs tend to be clustered in relatively low value-added sectors (e.g. trade, real estate) and face barriers to scale up their operations.

Environment and climate policy

Georgia has brought forward a range of environmental policies and strategies to support the greening of the economy and to meet international obligations. Among others, the government has identified investment needs of USD 8 billion to support energy efficiency and USD 2 billion for climate change adaptation, both types of investments are envisaged to be implemented by 2030. However, renewable and energy-efficiency laws and action plans remain under development and there are no binding renewable energy targets. Enforcement of environmental standards (e.g. buildings performance, pollution) lacks consistency. The specific role of SMEs in green growth and the barriers they face are generally not explicitly considered.

Georgia has a significant informal economy much of which occurs within the SME segment. Alongside creating fiscal and macro-economic challenges, the presence of a large informal economy also creates issues for effective environmental regulation. The formalisation of the economy should therefore be a priority for government.

Financing market for SMEs

Access to finance has been identified as a challenge for SMEs as is common elsewhere in the region. Commercial banks are the main source of SME finance, but the sector is regarded by lenders as relatively high risk. Interest rates tend to be relatively high (15%+), as are collateral requirements (130% and more). Rates offered in the microfinance sector are considerably higher. Borrowers often are already over-indebted or lack sufficient assets against which to borrow. Project finance approaches and leasing and factoring financial products also remain underdeveloped. Dollarisation of lending offers lower rates, but also creates potential risks for individual borrowers. The government is already actively working on addressing some of these risks.

Market gap for green SME investments

One key challenge facing green SMEs is the gap in the market in terms of green credit for SMEs from financial institutions. Many banks providing dedicated green credit lines tend to serve larger customers and loan sizes are often more than what an SME might need (e.g. loans >EUR 500 000). This reflects the commercial economies of scale and lower processing costs associated with larger loan-size portfolios. At the other end of the scale, microfinance organisations serve smaller SMEs (e.g. loans of up to EUR 10 000), but at significantly higher rates of interest. Indeed, many Georgian SMEs might be considered micro-SMEs. In addition, many energy and resource efficiency investments made by small firms (e.g. with typical loan sizes of EUR 10 000-30 000) are too big for microfinance institutions and too small for traditional bank lenders. This market gap requires special attention in government policies.

SME capacity challenges

Weak financial literacy, poor record keeping and business planning have constrained progress in building a market for green finance among SMEs. However, this has been improving. Borrowers may also lack awareness of the economic benefits of green investments. They may also have poor understanding of the potential paybacks, including productivity and quality benefits. Green investment may be regarded as an opportunity cost compared to expanding production.

Role of financial institutions

International financial institutions (IFIs) have already provided approximately USD 400 million in concessional credit lines to eight Georgian banks over the last decade for on-lending to green projects. These loans have primarily targeted renewable energy and energy efficiency. Of these banks, Bank of Georgia, TBC Bank and ProCredit Bank have been the most active in their support for green lending. Only ProCredit, however, has a sustained green lending product.

Barriers to access

IFI environmental credit lines provided to financial intermediaries have generally been allocated to larger companies and projects, with average loan sizes of USD 1 million. This reflects higher transaction costs of banks working with small borrowers, as well as poor alignment of IFI SME definitions with the Georgian context. Some credit lines have also been fungible between energy-efficiency and renewable energy projects. This has resulted in use of funds for hydropower rather than SME development.

Key success factors

Banks themselves have had to overcome capacity challenges to promote green lending. Any success can be attributed to a range of factors. These factors include senior management buy-in, development of standard green banking products, allocation of sufficient financial and staffing resources, a strong pipeline, economies of scale to offset potential transaction costs and a high level of transparency and governance.

Recommendations for policy makers

Significant economic and environmental benefits can be delivered through improving SME access to green finance given the important role played by small businesses in Georgia. Policy makers can support this process by addressing the following:

- Adopt pending legislation on energy efficiency and renewable energy, develop robust sub-regulation (buildings, appliances), strengthen enforcement, ratchet environmental standards and reduce fossil-fuel subsidies to create market signals.

- Ensure explicit policy consideration of the role of SMEs in the green transition and ensure that SME participation is included in national climate strategies and programmes.

- Address wider issues of access to finance for SMEs, including enabling access to credit at sub-national level, building SME financial literacy, exploring credit guarantees for SME lending and promoting non-bank financing (e.g. leasing).

- Lower cost of green credit and improve borrowing conditions for SMEs by working with national development funds and commercial banks to enhance interest rates and reduce collateral requirements.

- Improve the availability, efficiency and effectiveness of green finance through green bond markets, pooled climate finance vehicles and the judicious use of central banking regulation and reporting to promote sustainable asset allocation.

- Raise awareness among SMEs around energy-efficiency and renewable energy opportunities, support the uptake of energy management systems and promote the economic and commercial benefits of green investment and branding.

Chapter 1. The macroeconomic context for green investments in Georgia

This chapter briefly describes the macroeconomic and political context for green investments in Georgia with a focus on the investment climate. The general performance of the economy underpins the green finance needs and trends in the country. Throughout, seven figures examine trends over 2008-18. These include real gross domestic product growth rates, the GEL: USD exchange rate, the annual consumer inflation rate, the key monetary policy interest rate, gross fixed capital formation and foreign direct investment net inflows. It also includes Georgia's country ranking in the "Doing Business" report over that decade. The chapter finishes with some thoughts on how general improvements in the investment climate could contribute to higher levels of green finance, particularly in the energy sector.

1.1. Political context

Georgia has witnessed significant economic and political instability over recent years. In 2008, the territories of Abkhazia and South Ossetia established de facto independence from Georgia. Tbilisi has sought to integrate with Western blocs such as the North Atlantic Treaty Organization (NATO) and the European Union (EU). However, Georgia's geographic distance from Europe and its exposure to the Russian Federation (hereafter "Russia") has encouraged Tbilisi to seek supplementary partnerships with countries like Azerbaijan and Turkey.

Political rule has been broadly stable in Georgia. However, it must balance the often-competing challenges of democratic reform with the tendency towards consolidation of power by the ruling elites. In 2012, the Georgian Dream government came to power. It has won every subsequent election by a wide margin, defeating the United National Movement that governed between 2003-12.

In July 2016, the EU and Georgia Association Agreement (AA) (European Union, 2014[1]) provisionally applied the Deep and Comprehensive Free Trade Area (DCFTA)[1] arrangement as a preferential trade regime between the two sides. The EU is the main trade partner of Georgia. In 2018, around 27% of Georgia's trade took place with the EU, followed by Turkey (14%) and Russia (11%) (European Commission, 2019[2]).

1.2. Macroeconomic situation

Since the change of government in 2003, the country embarked on reforms to liberalise the economy. As a result, Georgia's economy has been growing steadily in recent years. Despite a sharp contraction in gross domestic product (GDP) in 2009 (as a result of the global financial crisis), Georgia has more recently posted steady economic growth of between 3-6% per annum (see Figure 1.1).

The most important sectors of the economy are agriculture, tourism, mining (manganese and copper) and manufacturing. Due to strained relations with Russia, Georgia has invested in energy independence by focusing on hydropower. The country is also attempting to use its key geographical location to become a logistics hub for gas and oil pipelines.

Figure 1.1. Real GDP growth rates 2008-18, annual percentage

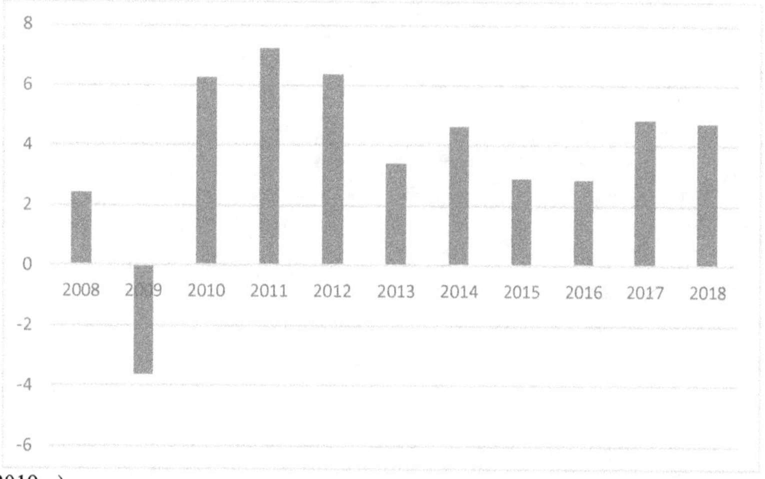

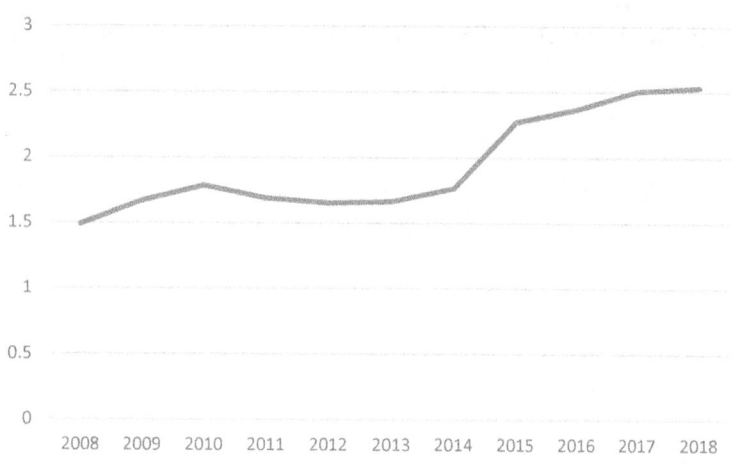

Source: (World Bank, 2019[3]).

The Georgian Lari (GEL) has been slowly depreciating against the US dollar (USD). The exchange rate stabilised between 2010-14, but has recently begun to depreciate further (see Figure 1.2).

Figure 1.2. GEL: USD Exchange rate, 2008-18

Source: (World Bank, 2019[3]).

The economy of Georgia has also benefited from relatively low interest rates from a regional perspective (see Figure 1.3), with a period of deflation in 2012-13.

Figure 1.3. Georgia annual consumer inflation, 2008-18, percentage

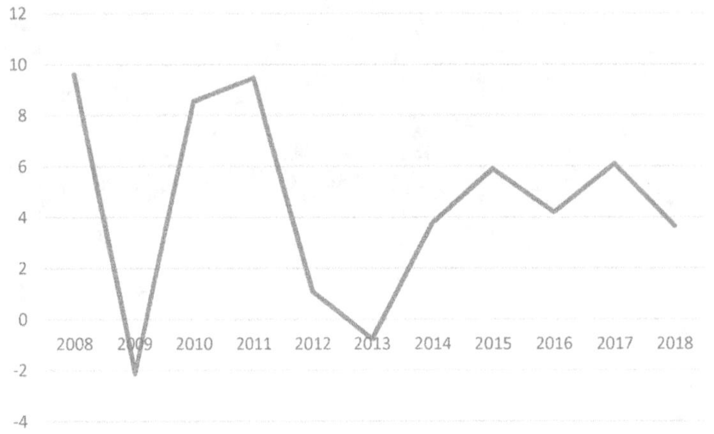

Source: (World Bank, 2019[3]).

Interest rates have been relatively low compared to other countries in the region over the same period. The key policy rate set by the National Bank of Georgia has fluctuated between 4-8%. This, in turn, has reduced the cost of borrowing in the real economy. High interest rates can reduce the capacity of borrowers to invest in energy efficiency and renewable energy (see Figure 1.4).

Figure 1.4. Georgia key monetary policy interest rate, 2008-18, percentage per annum

Source: (NBG, 2019[4]):

1.3. Macroeconomic situation

The investment climate in Georgia has been strengthened considerably over recent years. Significant anti-corruption efforts have mostly eradicated low-level bribery. Georgia ranks sixth in the 2018 World Bank "Doing Business" survey and is the highest placed country in the region. The government is focused on ensuring low deficit, inflation and a floating real exchange rate. However, attainment of these goals is affected by regional developments and other external factors. Public debt and deficits remain under control.

The 2014 medium-term economic strategy ("Georgia 2020") promotes business friendly policies and commitment to a low-taxation economy and investment in human capital. It also stresses the potential for trade and infrastructure development.

In 2012, the United States and Georgia established a High-Level Dialogue on Trade and Investment to identify ways of increasing bilateral trade and investment. In June 2014, Georgia signed an AA and DCFTA with the European Union.

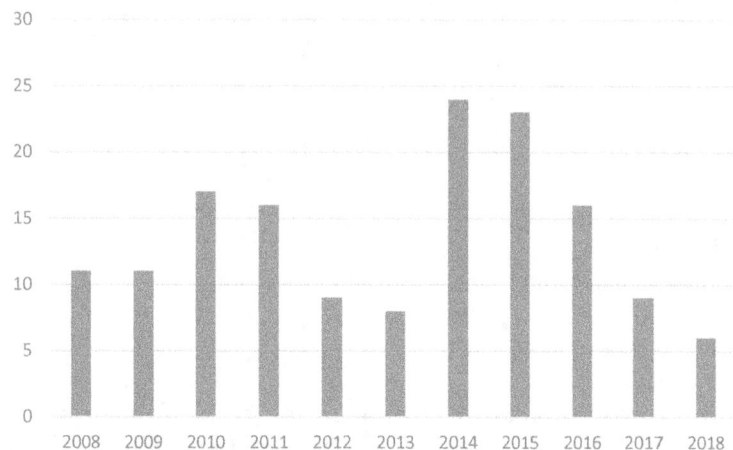

Figure 1.5. Georgia country ranking: "Doing Business" report 2008-18

Source: (World Bank, 2018[5]).

Gross fixed capital investment fell significantly in 2008-09. However, it returned to strong levels between 2016-18 at about 30% of GDP (see Figure 1.6).

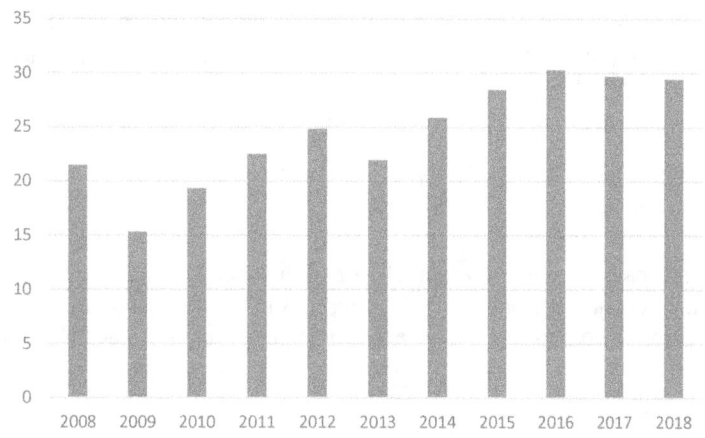

Figure 1.6. Gross fixed capital formation, share of GDP, 2008-18

Source: (World Bank, 2019[3]).

Foreign direct investment (FDI) has also recovered to pre-financial crisis levels as a share of GDP. However, it dropped significantly in 2018 (see Figure 1.7).

Figure 1.7. Foreign direct investment net inflows as a share of GDP, 2008-18

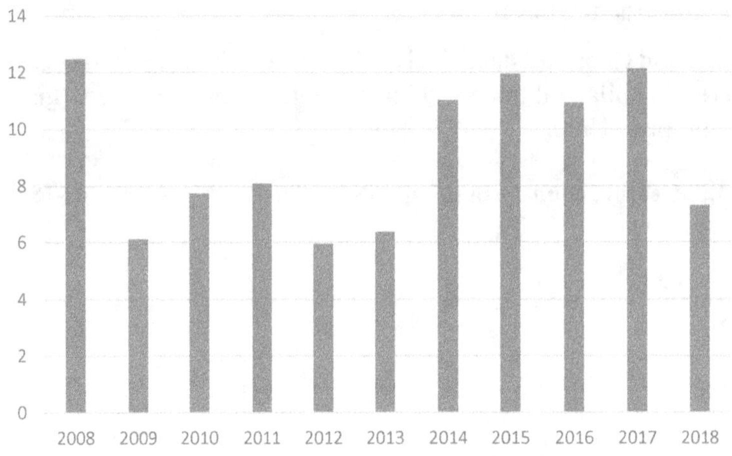

Source: (World Bank, 2019[3]):

1.4. Forward outlook

The Georgian economy continues to recover on the back of GDP growth and rising consumer demand. GDP is expected to grow in 2019 and inflation is expected to remain stable. The integration of Georgia's exports into the EU trade market is likely to increase the country's attractiveness as an investment destination.

Improvement in the investment climate is likely to result in a significant enabling effect on environmental investment, particularly in the energy sector. Reforms could potentially include significant strengthening of investment policy and investor protection to attract FDI and multi-national entities, and energising public-private dialogue within Georgia. To encourage private sector investment, Georgia may consider promoting environmental and climate-change disclosure requirements for private sector companies in line with standards of the EU and the Organisation for Economic Co-operation and Development.

Notes

[1] This agreement means both sides will mutually open their markets for goods and services based on predictable and enforceable trade rules. This is part of the broader Association Agreement whose political and co-operation components have been provisionally applied since November 2014.

References

European Commission (2019), "Countries and Regions, Georgia", webpage (accessed 23 October 2019), https://ec.europa.eu/trade/policy/countries-and-regions/countries/georgia/. [2]

European Union (2014), "Association Agreement between the European Union and the European Atomic Energy Community and their Member States, of the One Part, and Georgia, of the Other Part", *Official Journal of the European Union L 261/7*, Vol. 57/30 August, https://eeas.europa.eu/sites/eeas/files/association_agreement.pdf. [1]

NBG (2019), *Financial Soundness Indicators*, National Bank of Georgia, webpage (accessed 23 October 2019), https://www.nbg.gov.ge/index.php?m=304. [4]

World Bank (2019), *World Development Indicators*, (database) (accessed 23 September 2019), http://data.worldbank.org/products/wdi. [3]

World Bank (2018), *Doing Business 2019: Reforming to Create Jobs*, World Bank Group, Washington, DC, https://www.doingbusiness.org/content/dam/doingBusiness/media/Annual-Reports/English/DB2018-Full-Report.pdf. [5]

Chapter 2. Small and medium-sized enterprise policy in Georgia

This chapter analyses the environment for supporting small and medium-sized enterprise (SME) development in Georgia, including the importance of the informal sector and different definitions of SMEs. It provides an overview of the emerging policy context for economic development, including priorities for the Social-economic Development Strategy "Georgia 2020" and the National SME Development Strategy 2016-20. It analyses how the government is helping create an enabling environment for expansion of the sector through creation of the Georgian Enterprise Development Agency and Georgia's Innovation and Technology Agency. Finally, it identifies opportunities to align energy efficiency, renewable energy and SME sector development.

2.1. Context for SME development

The Georgian economy has typically been more structured around small and medium-sized enterprises (SMEs) and services than many other countries in the region. As a result, the profile of the economy is less carbon intensive than some other post-Soviet countries. In Ukraine or Belarus, for example, heavy industry continues to operate while Azerbaijan has an active upstream fossil-fuel industry.

Approximately 723 000 companies are registered in Georgia, of which around 25% are active. Using earlier Georgian definitions, of the total number of companies in Georgia, more than 85% were classified as small, with another 9% as medium. Trade and transport account for the largest volume of business turnover (47%) (USAID, 2017[1]).

In 2016, under the newly adopted European Union (EU) definition, SMEs accounted for 99.7% of all firms in the country (OECD, 2019[2]). However, many of these are rather micro and small companies (between 1-19 employees). SMEs are crucial for employment. More than half of all SMEs are estimated to be based in Tbilisi, with the remainder distributed mainly in the Imereti and Adjara regions. SMEs are an important source of economic activity in the Georgian economy. The National Statistics Office of Georgia estimates that SMEs provide more than 67% of employment and 61.5% of gross value added.

The informal economy in Georgia is also significant. A recent International Monetary Fund study estimates that the informal economy represented more than half of GDP in 2015, although this share has been decreasing steadily over time (Medina, L. and F. Schneider, 2018[3]). Much of the informal economy occurs within the SME segment. Alongside creating fiscal and macroeconomic challenges, the presence of a large informal economy also creates issues for effective environmental regulation. The formalisation of the economy should therefore be a priority for the government, including in terms of improving environmental performance among SMEs.

SMEs are struggling to scale their operations in Georgia. They tend to be clustered in relatively low value-added sectors (e.g. trade, real estate). Relatively few are in areas such as manufacturing. As a result, wages are also relatively low in the sector.

2.2. Definitions of SMEs in Georgia

Until recently, the Georgian Tax Code (President of Georgia, 2010[4]) and the Law on National Investment Agency (President of Georgia, 2002[5]) were used to define SMEs in Georgia and these definitions differed. The National Statistics Office of Georgia accounted for business using a different approach. In order to streamline these definitions, in March 2017, the National Statistics Office approved a new methodology for the SME registry. This new methodology became effective in 2018. For the sake of comparison, EU definition of SMEs is provided in Table 2.2.

Table 2.1. New Georgian definitions of SMEs

Category	No of employees	Average annual turnover (GEL)
Small	<50	<12 000 000
Medium	51-249	12-60 000 000
Large	>250	>60 000 000

Source: Information provided by the Ministry of Economy and Sustainable Development.

Table 2.2. EU definition of SMEs

Category	No of employees	Annual revenue (EUR)	Total assets (EUR)
Single entrepreneur/ micro	0-10	<2 000 000	<2 000 000
Small	11-50	<10 000 000	<10 000 000
Medium	51-250	<50 000 000	<43 000 000
Large	>250	>50 000 000	>43 000 000

Source: (European Commission, 2015[6]).

The classification of SMEs can affect where green finance is directed within the Georgian economy, particularly by international financial institutions (IFIs). For example, the Bank of Georgia uses different classification criteria. Companies with an annual turnover of GEL 1.5 million-20 million, or a loan exposure of USD 150 000-2 000 000 qualify as small and medium-sized companies in the Bank of Georgia classification.

Given the structure of the economy, many borrowers considered as corporate clients by local banks under the Georgian classification are considered eligible for SME under the EU/IFI definition. IFI credit lines tend to use international (e.g. EU) standards. As a result, Georgian banks have lent larger amounts to smaller numbers of corporate clients (e.g. loans of USD 1 million+) rather than focusing on smaller-scale SMEs in the Georgian context. Doing this reduces the transaction costs for Georgian banks but results in lower levels of green finance being accessible to micro and small businesses.

2.3. SME policy environment

The SME policy environment is generally considered to be well-developed and supportive in Georgia. The 2018 World Bank "Doing Business" survey ranked Georgia number 6 globally. The country has maintained its position among the highest placed of transition economies. In recent years, Georgia has sought to improve the business environment for all enterprises, including SMEs. It has simplified administrative regulations, reduced the tax burden, fought corruption, facilitated free trade and promoted privatisation. Among other measures, the Georgian government has put in place several regulations and institutions that support lending and borrowing. These aim to help improve access to credit (e.g. credit information system, central collateral registry, a civil code that allows for a wide range of assets to be pledged as collateral). Despite this favourable legal basis, access to finance remains a constraint for enterprises, particularly SMEs. This, in turn, hinders normal business operations and the transition to greener economic development.

In a 2016 study, the OECD developed an SME Policy Index looking at EU Eastern Partnership (EaP) countries analysing 12 dimensions/measures for implementing the Small Business Act (SBA) for Europe. Georgia received a positive review across seven of these measures, and was named as the best performing and reforming country among the EaP countries. It was praised for its work on insolvency, the regulation framework, support services for SMEs and start-ups, standards and technical regulations, and innovations. However, several challenges were identified, including access to finance and skills mismatch in the labour market and low-job creation.

The Social-economic Development Strategy "Georgia 2020" (Government of Georgia, 2014[7]) is a road map for the medium to long term, setting out the strategy, priorities and action plan by sector. It is strongly relevant to the development of the SME sector, identifying three main priority areas:

- Private sector competitiveness: improving the investment and business environment; promoting innovation and technology; facilitating the growth of exports; developing infrastructure and fully realising the country's transit potential

- Developing human resources: developing the country's workforce with a view to meeting labour market requirements; tightening the social security net; increasing the accessibility and quality of the country's healthcare system

- Access to finance: mobilising investments; developing financial intermediation.

Elsewhere, the government programme "Freedom, Rapid Development and Welfare" sets out support for SMEs in economic development, among other priorities. It promotes business start-ups and innovation under the economic reform thematic workstream.

2.4. National SME development strategy

In 2016, the Ministry of Economy and Sustainable Development (MESD) prepared and approved the National SME Development Strategy 2016-20 (Government of Georgia, 2015[8]). The strategy, developed in close cooperation with GIZ and OECD, forms the basis for SME sector development. Targets include increasing SME economic output by 10%, employment by 15% and manufacturing production by 7% over the duration of the strategy.

The National SME Strategy has five core thematic areas of focus:

- access to finance

- improvement of the institutional, legal and entrepreneurial environment

- SME skills and entrepreneurial culture development

- export support and SME internationalisation

- innovation and research development support.

For each thematic area, an action plan sets out short-term implementation measures. The first action plan was prepared for the period 2016-17. Support for SME development also forms part of a broad range of other strategies and policies:

- The Regional Development Programme of Georgia 2015-17 contains SME promotion and job creation as a core regional priority with links to specific sectors (e.g. tourism, agriculture).

- The Strategy for Agricultural Development in Georgia (2015-20) promotes the development of SMEs within the agriculture agenda.

- The Professional Education Reform Strategy 2013-20 recognises the need for capacity building and skills upgrade for the SME sector.

- The Deep and Comprehensive Free Trade Area (DCFTA) implementation action plan 2014-17 considers the role of SMEs, including access to finance and export promotion.

- The Rural Development Strategy 2017-20 and action plan, approved by the government in March 2017, also considers SMEs.

2.5. Institutional support

To support development of the SME sector, and to boost innovation and increase entrepreneurial activity, MESD has set up two agencies. These are the Georgian Enterprise Development Agency (Enterprise Georgia, 2019[9]) and Georgia's Innovation and Technology Agency (GITA, n.d.[10]).

- Georgian Enterprise Development Agency (EDA, or Enterprise Georgia) is the primary co-ordinator of programmes and policies to support SME sector development. It aims to support start-ups, improve competitiveness, build skills and help Georgia diversify its economic base with a view to promoting an export-led economy. To that end, it helps co-ordinate key state support programmes, promote better access to finance and offer consulting, capacity and business intelligence services. Enterprise Georgia has three main divisions:

    o The business division promotes entrepreneurial activity in Georgia by supporting entrepreneurs. It helps create new enterprises, as well as expand and refurbish existing ones.

    o The export division promotes the export potential of the country by increasing the competitiveness of local products and the overall volume of goods directed towards international markets.

    o The invest division attracts, promotes and develops foreign direct investment in Georgia. As the moderator between foreign investors and the government, the division ensures access to updated information, provides an efficient means of communication with government bodies and serves as a "one-stop-shop", supporting investors throughout the investment process.

- Georgia's Innovation and Technology Agency (GITA) co-ordinates and mediates innovation and technology development in Georgia. Its aims to provide a legal framework for innovation, support knowledge and innovation commercialisation, provide access to finance by grant programmes and create infrastructure for innovation. It also helps construct physical infrastructure for new technologies (e.g. techno-parks, innovation laboratories for start-ups, i-labs - innovation centres within universities), and foster dialogue between academia and industry. In addition, it promotes increased awareness around the role of innovation in the broader public.

In terms of professional associations, the sector is represented by a range of institutions. These include the Georgian Chamber of Commerce and Industry, Georgian Employers' Association and Georgian Small and Medium Enterprises Association.

A number of donors and IFIs also have programmes to support SME development. These include the World Bank, the European Bank for Reconstruction and Development (EBRD), the European Investment Bank (EIB), Deutsche Gesellschaft für Internationale Zusammenarbeit (GIZ), Kreditanstalt für Wiederaufbau (KfW), Asian Development Bank, United States Agency for International Development and Millennium Challenge Account.

2.6. Programmes and measures to support SMEs

Over recent years, three core national programmes have been established to support SME development in Georgia. These bring together a larger number of projects with a consolidated budget of about USD 100 million per annum.

- "Produce in Georgia" is developed by MESD and managed by EDA/Enterprise Georgia. Established in 2014, it supports the competitiveness of Georgian industry with a focus on building entrepreneurship among SMEs and export potential. As of June 2019, "Produce in Georgia" had supported 503 businesses with total investment value of Georgian lari (GEL) 1.18 billion (about USD 400 million) and had created more than 17 740 jobs. Much of this was invested in the field of agriculture and tourism/hotels (Enterprise Georgia, 2019[11]).

- GITA manages the implementation of innovation grant programmes. Mini grants and micro grants help Georgian companies and SMEs commercialise business ideas and technologies. (GITA, n.d.[10]). In the framework of a World Bank loan – Georgia National Innovation Ecosystem – GITA has launched a Startup Matching Grants Programme. This aims to support globally scalable start-ups, including in the field of green technology and agriculture, and improve their access to finance and access to global markets.

- The Ministry of Agriculture works through the Agricultural Projects Management Agency (APMA) to implement more than ten projects to support SME development in agriculture (APMA, 2019[12]).

In 2017, MESD reviewed the potential to unify these projects under a single branding and management structure "Produce in Georgia for Rapid Development".

2.7. Emerging measures

A range of emerging measures is under development as part of the draft National Strategy for SMEs:

- A draft of Innovative Georgia 2020 has been prepared and is expected to be supported by the World Bank's Innovation Development Project.

- Changes to Georgian definitions of SMEs are expected to align them with EU standards. This can result in a significantly higher proportion of the economy being classified as SMEs compared to previous Georgian standards.

2.8. Barriers to access to finance

The government of Georgia has made significant progress to support development of a vibrant SME sector. Achievements include reducing barriers to entry, simplifying business registration, lowering taxes, and supporting a robust regulatory environment.

However, access to finance remains a key barrier to SME growth. Smaller SMEs are less likely to access international finance. They typically face higher costs than large enterprises and similar companies in comparable countries. Some key barriers are set out below:

- Commercial banks are the main source of funding for SMEs in Georgia. In general, lenders regard the SME sector as being relatively high risk. Smaller SME borrowers tend to lack the collateral or track record to engage with the banking sector. They may also be already over-borrowed, thereby creating less capacity for further credit expansion. Georgian banks are keen to manage their exposure to non-performing loans. They are highly sensitive to robust balance sheets and strong capital adequacy ratios, particularly banks with an international shareholder base.

- Burdensome collateral requirements are a significant barrier. In terms of collateral, banks may sometimes demand more than 130% of the total loan value (usually in the form of real estate or land). For many SMEs, this is challenging as their fixed asset base may be relatively small, or their value proposition based around intangible assets.

- High interest rates, especially in local currency, also create significant barriers for many SMEs in Georgia to access finance. Interest rates for loans are generally high (about 23% for individual entrepreneurs and 16% for legal entities), reflecting the relatively high levels of perceived risk. Rates are significantly higher for borrowers using microfinance structures. As a result, SMEs face a significant financing gap.

- The length (or tenor) of finance on offer can also be a constraint. Often maturities are relatively short. They may not reflect the potential payback periods needed for profitable capital investment (e.g. renewable energy or energy efficiency).

- Loan dollarisation is also an issue from an interest rate perspective. Over the last five years, many SMEs have sought to borrow in foreign currency due to the lower headline interest rates. However, this means that SMEs are not hedged against local currency fluctuation and exchange rate effect. A weakening local currency (as has been the case in Georgia over recent years) results in a real-term increase in the value of loans.

- Banks also view low levels of financial capacity and understanding among SMEs as a key issue in terms of providing access to finance and pricing loans. Weak financial record keeping and business planning prevent lending. However, this has been improving over recent years as the Georgian economy has liberalised and matured.

- Banks also tend to have a more centralised credit system in Georgia, thereby creating some challenges for regional lending to SMEs. Regional loan officers may not be well-trained to assess SME risks or authorised to make lending decisions.

- There is limited availability of alternative non-bank and equity-financing mechanisms. Asset-based finance, such as leasing and factoring, is underused. As well, the venture-capital environment is at a nascent stage. A recent Law on Collective Investment Undertakings (President of Georgia, 2013[13]) defines venture capital and private equity funds. However, venture capital activities and awareness of business angels remain low.

SME access to credit in Georgia is not significantly out of line compared to other countries. A World Bank/EBRD survey on business environment and enterprise performance in

Georgia identifies low wealth and high levels of corporate debt rather than bank-lending policies as the key constraints to SME lending (GET Georgia, 2018[14]). The share of SME credit has been increasing over the past two years in Georgia.

2.9. Financing structures

The government has tried to address barriers to access finance. Targeted programmes aim to provide access to credit under the SME support programmes previously identified. These programmes provide a range of instruments. Some provide grants, while others subsidise the interest rate for SME beneficiaries. However, this does not address the issue of collateral, making it challenging for some smaller SMEs to participate.

To address this challenge, the government recently introduced a new credit guarantee scheme which aims to tackle specific market failures, and support risk diversification and credit supply growth. The budget for this initial stage of the scheme is GEL 20 million (about USD 7 million) and it can be further expanded in the future. It is a pilot phase that the government can learn from and adjust later on accordingly. This mechanism will give access to finance to SMEs with insufficient collateral for securing bank loans or that operate in a sector or market considered high risk by the banking sector credit policy.

Examples of other support measures are set out below:

- Under "Produce in Georgia", if a company gets a loan from the bank, the government can finance part of the interest payment. The loan amount needs to be between USD 150 000–2 000 000 for manufacturing projects and USD 600 000–2 000 000 for agricultural projects. Interest rates are between 11-13% and the government co-finance amount is 10% (only for the first 24 months). As one stipulation, 80% of the loan should purchase capital assets.

- The Ministry of Agriculture and 11 major banks have been running a subsidised agro-credit programme since 2013. The APMA subsidises part of the loan interest payments. Rates are subsidised by 11% for capital asset investments (USD 12 000–600 000) and 8% for working capital (GEL 2 000–100 000, or USD 740–37 000). The ministry also offers grants for agro-processors for capital asset investment or training of up to GEL 500 000 (USD 186 000) and 40% of total project value.

- Under the "Host in Georgia" programme, the government provides a 10% interest rate for GEL-denominated loans and 8% for loans in USD/EUR. The interest rate co-financing lasts for two years. The minimum amount is GEL 500 000 (USD 186 000). The government also provides a collateral guarantee for 50% of the total loan for the first four years. In addition, it co-finances franchising/management agreement fees of GEL 300 000 (USD 112 000) annually for the first two years.

- Under the GITA mini grants programme, SMEs can access grants of up to GEL 100 000 (about USD 35 000) to support commercialisation, and under the micro grants programme up to GEL 5 000 (about USD 1 900).

- The World Bank project proposes matching grants of between USD 30 000–250 000, requiring some level of co-financing for innovation.

2.10. Market gap for green SME investments

A key challenge facing green SMEs in particular is the gap in the market in terms of financial institutions offering green credit for micro and small-sized firms. Many of the existing banks providing dedicated green credit lines tend to serve larger SME customers and loan sizes are often larger (e.g. >EUR 100 000) than might be required for a typical energy or resource efficiency investment by an SME (between EUR 10 000 and 30 000 but often closer to the lower boundary, see Annex B for examples of typical resource efficient investments made by small businesses). On the other end of the market, micro-finance organisations serve smaller SMEs but at significantly higher interest rates. This gap in the market of green finance is a significant constraint to increasing energy and resource efficiency investments by small firms. In other words, such investments are too big for microfinance institutions and too small for traditional bank lenders. This market gap requires special attention in government policies.

References

APMA, N. (2019), "Agricultural and Rural Development Agency", webpage (accessed 23 September 2019), http://apma.ge/. [12]

Enterprise Georgia (2019), "Results of the Micro and Small Business Support Component", webpage (accessed 23 September 2019), http://www.enterprisegeorgia.gov.ge/en/News/results-of-the-micro-and-small-8. [9]

Enterprise Georgia (2019), "Results of the State Program 'Produce in Georgia'", webpage (accessed 23 September 2019), http://www.enterprisegeorgia.gov.ge/en/News/results-of-the-state-program-p. [11]

European Commission (2015), *User Guide to the SME Definition*, European Commission, Brussels, http://ec.europa.eu/growth/content/revised-user-guide-sme-definition-0_en. [6]

Georgia, G. (2016), *Freedom, Rapid Development, Prosperity, Government Platform 2016-2020*, Government of Georgia, Tbilisi, http://gov.ge/files/41_61087_816118_GoG_Platform_LKF_19_05_2017.pdf. [15]

GET Georgia (2018), "Banking sector monitoring Georgia 2018", *Policy Study Series*, No. PS/01, German Economic Team Georgia/Berlin Economics, Tibilisi/Berlin, https://www.get-georgia.de/wp-content/uploads/2018/03/PS_01_2018_en.pdf. [14]

GITA (n.d.), "Georgia's Innovation and Technology Agency", webpage (accessed 23 September 2019), https://gita.gov.ge/eng. [10]

Government of Georgia (2015), *SME Development Strategy of Georgia, 2016-2020*, Government of Georgia, Tbilisi, http://www.economy.ge/uploads/files/2017/ek__politika/eng_sme_development_strategy.pdf. [8]

Government of Georgia (2014), *Social-economic Development Strategy of Georgia: Georgia 2020*, Government of Georgia, Tbilisi, https://policy.asiapacificenergy.org/sites/default/files/Georgia%202020_ENG.pdf. [7]

Medina, L. and F. Schneider (2018), "Shadow economies around the world: What did we learn over the last 20 years?", *Working Paper*, No. 18/17, International Monetary Fund, Washington, DC, https://www.imf.org/en/Publications/WP/Issues/2018/01/25/Shadow-Economies-Around-the-World-What-Did-We-Learn-Over-the-Last-20-Years-45583. [3]

NAMA (2017), *Georgia – NAMA*, Nationally Appropriate Mitigation Actions, Georgia (database) (accessed 23 October 2019), http://www.nama-database.org/index.php/Georgia. [16]

OECD (2019), *Financing SMEs and Entrepreneurs 2019: An OECD Scoreboard*, OECD Publishing, Paris, https://dx.doi.org/10.1787/fin_sme_ent-2019-en. [2]

President of Georgia (2013), *Law of Georgia on Collective Investment Undertakings, 24 July 2013, No 843-ES*, President of Georgia, Tbilisi, https://matsne.gov.ge/en/document/download/1981090/4/en/pdf. [13]

President of Georgia (2010), *Law of Georgia on Tax Code of Georgia, 17 September 2010 , No 3 591-IIS,*, President of Georgia, Tbilisi, https://matsne.gov.ge/en/document/download/1043717/93/en/pdf. [4]

President of Georgia (2002), *Law of Georgia on the Georgian National Investment Agency No 519 of 19 June 2002, last amended on 4 March 2015*, President of Georgia, Tbilisi, https://matsne.gov.ge/en/document/download/2763422/0/en/pdf. [5]

USAID (2017), *Innovation and Technology in Georgia*, United States Agency for International Development, Washington, DC. [1]

Chapter 3. Energy, Environmental and Climate Policy of Georgia

This chapter looks at the sustainable energy and climate policy in Georgia, and the emerging policy context for green investment, particularly for small and medium-sized enterprises. This includes key strategic documents such as the Low Emission Development Strategy and Nationally Appropriate Mitigation Actions. It also includes emerging policy documents such as the National Energy Efficiency Action Plan and National Renewable Energy Action. After reviewing the most recent relevant policy developments, the chapter concludes with a discussion of potential areas that need further strengthening. Relevant themes include renewable energy targets, environmental regulations and enforcement, energy prices, public procurement and non-renewable energy options.

3.1. Context

The energy intensity of the Georgian economy is high, particularly in industrial facilities and small and medium-sized enterprises (SMEs). Environmental concerns have been part of the government agenda for several years. These are reflected in a range of policy documents set out in Table 3.1.

The Socio-Economic Development Strategy "Georgia 2020" adopted in 2014 highlights three key principles of economic development. These comprise the rational use of natural resources, ensuring environmental safety and sustainability (Government of Georgia, 2014[1]).

In terms of climate action, Georgia has communicated its climate targets internationally through its Intended Nationally Determined Contribution (INDC) (Government of Georgia, 2015[2]), (FAO, 2018[3]). The country is working on a more ambitious NDC document, which it plans to submit by the end of 2020. It has also developed key strategic documents such as the Low Emission Development Strategy (LEDS) and Nationally Appropriate Mitigation Actions (NAMAs) (NAMA, 2017[4]), among others. While the LEDS document has been prepared, the government has not yet adopted it. In addition, several cities and municipalities have made commitments under the Covenant of Mayors (Covenant of Mayors, 2017[5]), and 11 have developed voluntary Sustainable Energy Action Plans (SEAPs).

Georgia is also mainstreaming climate and environment considerations into wider economic development policy.[1] These include a Green Economy Strategy, led by the Ministry of Economy and Sustainable Development (MESD). The 2016 Green Growth Policy Paper, developed in co-operation with GIZ, set out pathways for development of this strategy. Analytical work to support the strategy considers three main sectors (buildings, agriculture and tourism) and their interlinkages (UN Environment, 2018[6]). MESD plans to further elaborate the Green Growth Policy Paper, including the strategy and an accompanying action plan.

The National Energy Efficiency Action Plan (NEEAP) also remains under development. The draft plan for 2017–20 set out overall energy efficiency targets, as well as sectoral targets for buildings, industry and transport. As adoption was delayed, the initial period covered by the plan is no longer relevant. At the request of the Ministry of Finance, MESD is preparing an update for NEEAP to 201922. MESD is also leading the development of a National Renewable Energy Action Plan (NREAP).

The government has authority to adopt NEEAP and NREAP, while Parliament is responsible for adopting laws on energy efficiency and renewable energy. All documents have been submitted to the relevant authorities, but adoption is still pending.

Table 3.1. Overview of relevant energy and environmental policy development in Georgia

Name	Scope	Status	Notes
Nationally Determined Contribution	National	Submitted to UNFCCC in 2015	Communicates Georgia's climate-related targets internationally
Georgia 2020	National	Adopted in 2014	Identifies priorities and problems to be dealt with to achieve long-term, sustainable and inclusive economic growth, including renewable energy and energy efficiency
Climate Change Strategy	National	Adopted in 2014	Aims to identify feasible ways to reduce the vulnerability of ecosystems and GHG emissions from various emitting sectors
Main Directions of the State Policy in the Energy Sector	National/ sectoral	Adopted in 2007, amended in 2015	Sets the enhanced use of renewable energy sources as a national policy
Law on Electricity and Natural Gas	National/ sectoral	Adopted in 1999, amended in 2013	Supports priority use of local hydro and other renewable, alternative and gas resources
State Programme "Renewable Energy 2008"	National/ sectoral	Adopted in 2008, amended in 2013	Specifies rules and procedures for development of renewable energy sources
Low Emission Development Strategy	National	Draft finished as of August 2017	Identifies sectoral strategies and goals to achieve low-carbon development pathways
National Energy Efficiency Action Plan	National	Finalised, and seeking government approval as of June 2017	Identifies energy emission targets, policy measures and financial needs
Nationally Appropriate Mitigation Actions (NAMAs)	Sectoral	Finalised	Developed NAMAs on biomass energy, buildings, sustainable forest management, transport and hydropower
National Forestry Concept for Georgia	Sectoral	Approved in 2013	Serves as a basis for sustainable development of forest management and related policy frameworks
Sustainable Energy Action Plans (SEAPs) under the Covenant of Mayors	Municipal	11 SEAPs have been approved and submitted as of 2018	Shows the individual signatory municipalities' commitments to voluntarily reducing GHG emissions
Tbilisi Sustainable Urban Transport Strategy	Municipal/ sectoral	Finalised in 2016	Defines policy directions and priorities on sustainable transport to be implemented between 2015 and 2030
Green Economy Concept	National/ sectoral	Under development	This will develop green economy interventions in various sectors, which can also lead to higher income and employment
Green City Action Plan of Tbilisi	Municipal	Under development	This will present benchmarking and priorities for tasks and defines the long-term Green City vision – within a timeframe of 10-15 years – supported by the European Bank for Reconstruction and Development
National Adaptation Plan	National	Under development	The first draft will focus on the agriculture sector
National Renewable Energy Action Plan	National	Finalised in 2018 and submitted to the government	This plan has developed a national policy framework for renewable energy sources, which is also compatible with Renewable Energy Directive 2009/28/EC
Georgia's Country Programme with the Green Climate Fund	National	Finalised, under procedural approval process at Ministry of Env Protection and Agriculture	Georgia's Country Programme with the Green Climate Fund analyses key national climate change strategies and actions and serves as an instrument to synthesise project ideas on climate change – both mitigation, adaptation and cross-cutting issues – to identify and present those ideas most suitable for Green Climate Fund funding
Climate Action Plan	National	Under development	The Ministry of Environmental Protection and Agriculture is developing this plan as an INDC implementation strategy

Source: Adapted from (OECD, 2018[7]) and updated by the authors.

In addition, the Ministry of Environmental Protection and Agriculture has been preparing a Climate Action Plan as part of the NDC implementation strategy. This includes concrete steps and figures for achieving climate-related targets. Further detail is provided below.

Intended nationally determined contribution

Through the INDC, Georgia commits 15% of greenhouse gas (GHG) emission reductions below business as usual (BAU) by 2030. Further, it has committed 25% of reductions below BAU, contingent on international support with finance and technology (approximately 41% below 1990 benchmark levels) (Government of Georgia, 2015[2]). The INDC does not, however, quantify the volume of finance necessary to deliver on these targets.

The INDC describes Georgia's national targets on climate change mitigation and adaptation by 2030. It does not include details on proposed actions, or a robust examination of financial needs, to achieve the targets. Instead, the INDC refers to the Low Emission Development Strategy (LEDS) and the National Energy Efficiency Action Plan (NEEAP).

Low Emission Development Strategy

Georgia finalised its LEDS in the middle of 2017. It was prepared under the Enhancing Capacity for Low Emission Development Strategies Program with support of the United States Agency for International Development (USAID, 2017[8]). LEDS aims to support Georgia's transition to a low-emission economy through various approaches, including the following:

- identifying main sources of GHG emissions and their future trajectories
- setting goals and needed policy measures to tackle barriers to reducing GHG emissions in the selected sectors
- outlining necessary legislation systems, infrastructure and co-ordination for implementation
- proposing mechanisms to mobilise the national and international financial sources for implementation of LEDS (Winrock and Remissia, 2017[9]).

National Energy Efficiency Action Plan

The government prepared the NEEAP between 2015-17 (NEEAP Expert Team, 2017[10]). The NEEAP sets out detailed plans for energy efficiency, such as a financing scheme, energy auditing and performance labelling, as well as sector-specific measures. The latter includes measures on buildings, public bodies, industry, transport, heating and cooling, and energy transformation, transmission, distribution and demand response.

Energy community

Georgia has been one of the Energy Community Contracting Parties since July 2017 (Energy Community Secretariat, 2017[11]). The need to comply with several relevant European Union (EU) directives over time is likely to result in higher support for renewable energy and energy-efficiency investments in Georgia. These include Directive 2012/27/EU on Energy Efficiency, Directive 2010/30/EU on Labelling and Standard Product Information on the Consumption of Energy and Other Resources (due on 31 December 2018) and Directive 2010/31/EU on Energy Performance of Buildings (30 June 2019).

Nationally appropriate mitigation actions

Georgia has also developed a number of Nationally Appropriate Mitigation Actions (NAMAs). These are meant to be linked to and aligned with the NEEAP. Among these are NAMAs focused on clean energy production, energy-efficient refurbishment of public buildings and use of biomass for rural development (NAMA, 2017[4]).

3.2. Renewable energy

The use of renewable energy sources is set as a key national priority in Main Directions of State Policy in the Energy Sector (Government of Georgia, 2017[12]). Relevant frameworks support infrastructure, finance and research. Georgia has also developed specific legal frameworks to support hydropower development.

MESD is working with the United Nations Development Programme (UNDP) to develop a NREAP. This is because legal frameworks on renewable energy in Georgia do not fully comply with the Renewable Energy Directive 2009/28/EC in light of the EU-Georgia Association Agreement and the Energy Community Treaty.

3.3. Potential areas for strengthening

While Georgia has made much progress in certain areas such as hydropower development, it is not necessarily a front-runner in the field of energy efficiency or other types of renewable energy. Other countries in Eastern Europe and Caucasus or in Central Europe with similar levels of gross domestic product per capita (purchasing power parity) often have stronger policies, especially for energy efficiency [see (Energy Community, 2019[13]) for an overview of regional policies].

Therefore, several policy areas could potentially be strengthened to improve the likelihood of green investment in the SME sector as previously set out by the Organisation for Economic Co-operation and Development (OECD, 2018[7]).

- More robust targets: Georgia is the only country in the Eastern Europe, Caucasus and Central Asia region, except Turkmenistan, not to have yet adopted any quantitative targets for renewable energy or energy efficiency into legislation.

- Environmental regulations: According to the United Nations Industrial Development Organization and from discussions with representatives of the business community, Georgian enterprises consider environmental policies and enforcement to be the most important driver for investment in energy efficiency and cleaner production. They believe such policies may create economic opportunities for new market development.

- Higher energy prices: Low energy prices still make small-scale renewables relatively uncompetitive and impede investments in energy efficiency. Raising energy prices and removing subsidies would lead companies to respond by improving efficiency and productivity.

- Strengthening regulation and enforcement: Growth-oriented policies are often seen as having been at the expense of weaker standards on energy use and environmental performance. Despite growing evidence to the contrary (OECD, 2017[14]), some government stakeholders continued to identify environmental improvement with creating negative impacts on growth. This is reflected in the relatively loose

- Finalisation and alignment of policy frameworks: Georgia has a range of frameworks guiding mitigation and energy-efficiency policy at the national and sectoral level (NEEAP, LEDS, INDC). The adoption of pending policies and strategies and the incorporation of energy-efficiency performance or other environmental considerations could help build SME markets for green goods and services.

- Greening public procurement: Public procurement rules can potentially contribute to creating significant demand by public bodies for low-carbon, climate-resilient goods and services.

- Promotion of non-hydro renewable energy options: Hydropower investment has been robust, but there has been little progress on other types of renewable energy. This is especially true for smaller building-scale technologies that might interest SMEs. The government could consider how differentiated support might help grow the market for alternative technologies.

Notes

[1] See OECD (2018), "Green Finance and Investment. Mobilising Finance for Climate Action in Georgia" for a full overview on the emerging policy and financing context for green investment.

References

Covenant of Mayors (2017), *Covenant of Mayors – Signatories*, http://www.covenantofmayors.eu/about/about/. [5]

Energy Community (2019), "Energy Community", webpage (accessed 23 September 2019), https://www.energy-community.org. [13]

Energy Community Secretariat (2017), *Energy Governance in Georgia, Report on Compliance with the Energy Community Acquis*, Energy Community Secretariat, Vienna, http://www.euneighbours.eu/sites/default/files/publications/2017-08/ECS_Georgia_Report_082017.pdf. [11]

FAO (2018), *Policy Analysis of Nationally Determined Contributions in Europe and Central Asia,*, Food and Agriculture Organization of the United Nations, Rome, http://www.fao.org/3/ca2684en/CA2684EN.pdf. [3]

Government of Georgia (2017), *Main Directions of the State Policy in Energy Sector of Georgia*, Government of Georgia, Tbilisi, http://www.energy.gov.ge/projects/pdf/pages/MAIN%20DIRECTIONS%20OF%20THE%20STATE%20POLICY%20IN%20ENERGY%20SECTOR%20OF%201047%20eng.pdf. [12]

Government of Georgia (2015), *Georgia's Intended Nationally Determined Contribution*, United Nations Framework Convention on Climate Change, Bonn, http://www4.unfccc.int/submissions/INDC/Published%20Documents/Georgia/1/INDC_of_Georgia.pdf. [2]

Government of Georgia (2014), *Social-economic Development Strategy of Georgia: Georgia 2020*, Government of Georgia, Tbilisi, https://policy.asiapacificenergy.org/sites/default/files/Georgia%202020_ENG.pdf. [1]

NAMA (2017), *Georgia – NAMA*, Nationally Appropriate Mitigation Actions, Georgia (database) (accessed 23 October 2019), http://www.nama-database.org/index.php/Georgia. [4]

NEEAP Expert Team (2017), *Draft National Energy Efficiency Action Plan, Report Commissioned by EBRD*, National Energy Efficiency Action Plan, Tbilisi. [10]

OECD (2018), *Mobilising Finance for Climate Action in Georgia*, Green Finance and Investment, OECD Publishing, Paris, https://dx.doi.org/10.1787/9789264289727-en. [7]

OECD (2017), *Investing in Climate, Investing in Growth*, OECD Publishing, Paris, https://dx.doi.org/10.1787/9789264273528-en. [14]

UN Environment (2018), *Supporting the Development of a Green Growth Strategy in Georgia*, United Nations Environment Programme, Geneva-Tbilisi, http://www.green-economies-eap.org/resources/Georgia%20GE%20report%20ENG%2027%20Jun.pdf. [6]

USAID (2017), "Georgia Overview", Enhancing Capacity for Low-Emission Development Strategies, archived webpage (accessed 23 October 2019), https://www.ec-leds.org/countries/georgia. [8]

Winrock and Remissia (2017), *Georgia Low Emission Development Strategy Draft Report*, commissioned by the USAID-funded EC-LEDS Clean Energy Program, Winrock International and Sustainable Development Center, Little Rock, US. [9]

Chapter 4. Climate finance for SMEs in Georgia

This chapter analyses the provision of green finance to small and medium-sized enterprises (SMEs) in Georgia. It discusses the experience of three banks most active in the Georgian market – Bank of Georgia, ProCredit Bank Georgia and TBC Bank. On this basis, the chapter discusses the sustainable energy challenges in Georgia, and the emerging policy context for green investment. These are analysed in terms of supply-side and demand-side policy measures. The chapter finishes by identifying possible policy responses to scale up green finance for SMEs in the country.

4.1. Overview

There are a number of estimates at the national level of financing requirements for Georgia to meet its sustainable development and climate change targets. However, these do not specifically refer to small and medium-sized enterprises (SMEs). Estimates include the following:

- USD 8.3 billion for 2017-30 for energy efficiency (National Energy Efficiency Action Plan) (NEEAP Expert Team, 2017[1])

- USD 10.6 billion between 2017-30 for energy efficiency, non-energy greenhouse gas (GHG) and land use, land-use change, and forestry emission reduction (Low Emission Development Strategy) (Winrock and Remissia, 2017[2])

- USD 2.4 billion for hydropower 2017-30 (Third National Communication of Georgia to the United Nations Framework Convention on Climate Change) (Government of Georgia, 2015[3])

- USD 1.5-2.0 billion for climate change adaptation over 2021-30 (Intended Nationally Determined Contribution) (Government of Georgia, 2015[4])

A significant proportion of these financial flows is not directly relevant to SMEs. However, sufficient funds should be accessible to, and affordable for, Georgian SMEs. This would allow them to invest in green projects (e.g. energy efficiency, renewable energy sources). It would also help them develop the market for provision of green goods and services (e.g. energy-efficient building products). Green technologies are expensive and, in Georgia, about 90% of these technologies are imported[1]. Much can be done by both the government (e.g. making energy-efficiency standards mandatory, introducing tax relief on certain technologies) and the international community (e.g. international financial institutions can offer more diversified financial mechanisms rather than just loans) to make green technologies more affordable. Improving the availability and affordability of green investment will also reduce waste and transition SMEs towards more efficient and modern technologies. This, in turn, would help improve wider productivity and innovation in the Georgian economy.

The scope of "green finance" in this report refers to those investments that provide environmental benefits in the broader context of environmentally sustainable development such as investments in clean / renewable sources of energy, energy efficiency, reductions in air, water and land pollution, recycling and waste management, and clean transport. The European Union (EU) is currently developing EU Taxonomy of Sustainable Activities[2], a classification of agreed definitions and terms of sustainable development types of projects which can qualify as green investments. This Taxonomy is expected to clarify many issues that bankers and investors have with regard to green investments and finance.

4.2. Georgian credit market

Retail lending has been one of the main drivers behind credit growth but due to recent regulatory changes the share of lending to SMEs and corporates has significantly increased. Corporate lending is constrained by existing indebtedness among corporate clients and the ability of larger firms to access cheaper international funding. Bank lending appears to work well, although capital market instruments remain underdeveloped.

In terms of access to credit, the credit ratio to gross domestic product (GDP) is relatively high compared to other countries in the region. Growth in credit is higher than GDP growth and has increased over recent years.

Figure 4.1. Growth in credit vs GDP growth in Georgian banks, share per annum, 2012-18

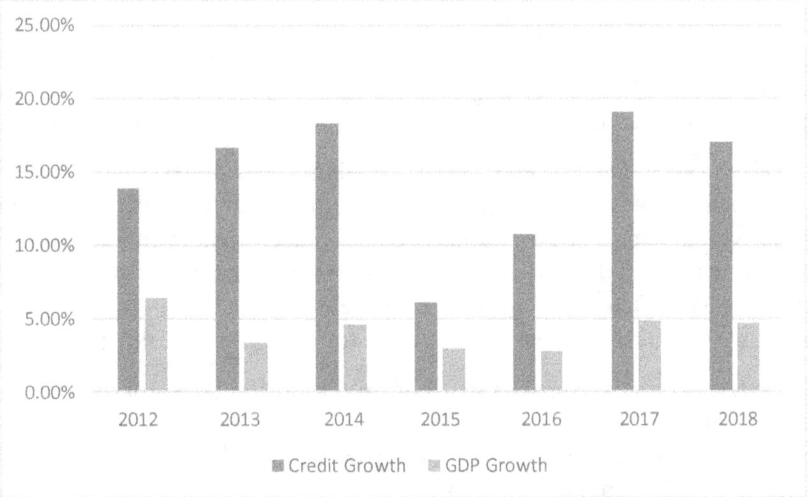

Source: (NBG, 2019[5]).

Loan growth (both real and adjusted for the exchange rate) is generally higher than economic growth. There is an ongoing availability and volume of credit relative to GDP. Aggregate demand is the driving force for credit expansion with no evidence of a credit crunch (sharp reduction in credit availability).

Retail credit is one of the main drivers of loan growth (with a 20% year-on-year increase). The National Bank of Georgia (NBG) is addressing emerging risks to complement its dedollarisation strategy (e.g. limits on loan-to-value ratios). Retail credit penetration (32% of GDP) is relatively high. While concerns exist around rapid growth, safeguards appear to be in place. Retail loans represent 55% of credit in 2017, compared to 49% in 2014.

SME lending and access to finance has been flagged as the third most important obstacle to business (EBRD/World Bank Group, 2015[6]). However, the share of SMEs identifying this barrier is similar to other countries. SME credit as a share of overall corporate credit has been increasing over the last two years. Retail access to credit is also in line with other countries. The main issues relating to access to finance appear to be low levels of SME wealth/assets and existing indebtedness rather than bank lending policies per se.

There have been significant declines in interest rates on loans denominated in both GEL and foreign currencies, as well as in the loan-deposit spreads for both. Despite high levels of return on equity, banks do appear to be passing through economic gains into more competitive loan pricing. At present, GEL-USD interest rate spreads are the main driver of dollarisation. In the meantime, many SMEs have been happy to access foreign currency loans at lower interest rates, despite the currency exposure this can bring.

4.3. Green credit

To some extent, green finance is already available to support investment in energy, resource efficiency and green supply chains among Georgian SMEs. Credit lines, extended by international financial institutions (IFIs) and disbursed through local banks, are the main source of long-term financing for green investments for SMEs in Georgia and across the wider EU's Eastern Partnership (EaP) countries (OECD, 2016[7]). At least eight banks and microfinance institutions have benefited from such IFI credit lines in Georgia.

Local banks on-lend to private sector clients (households, SMEs, larger industrial companies and renewable energy project developers). The end user and the local bank can often benefit from consultancy services and training to develop feasible projects.3

The tenor of the credit lines offered by IFIs is also often longer than that available to banks on the local market. Being able to match maturities and benefit from cheaper cost of capital provides some comfort to local banks, making them more willing to lend. Such credit lines facilitate access to longer-term finance that might otherwise be unavailable to SMEs. They also make it more feasible for these companies to borrow over timescales that match the payback periods for energy-efficiency investments.

In terms of interest rates, the cost of loans offered to SMEs does not directly reflect the cost of IFI credit lines. Loans are generally priced dynamically based on a borrower credit assessment and competition in the wider lending market. High cost of capital can make investments with potentially negative marginal abatement costs4 more expensive, thereby reducing the attractiveness of such investments to borrowers.

Most IFIs active in the region have opened environmental credit lines with local financing institutions (FIs). In Georgia, the primary IFIs involved have included the European Bank for Reconstruction and Development (EBRD), the European Investment Bank (EIB), KfW (Germany), the Development Bank of Austria (OeEB). Two multilateral facilities (Green for Growth Fund (GGF) and the Global Climate Partnership Fund (GCPF) have also played important roles. The Green Climate Fund (GCF) has provided funds to EBRD for on-lending through the Sustainable Lending Financing Facility.

Box 4.1. IFIs involved in green financing in Georgia

More detail on the IFIs that have set up environmental credit lines in Georgia is provided below:

- EBRD has operated a series of credit lines to six Georgian banks. Most recently under the EnergoCredit brand, EBRD provided a USD 125 million credit line programme to banks in the Caucasus region between 2007-17. Partner banks included Bank of Georgia (BoG), Bank Republic (later acquired by TBC Bank), BasisBank, Credo Bank, TBC Bank and VTB Bank. In 2016, the Green Climate Fund agreed to a large energy-efficiency financing facility with EBRD of USD 375 million. It will support lending through financial intermediaries in ten countries alongside USD 1 billion of EBRD co-financing. In addition, in 2017, EBRD provided credit lines to BoG and TBC

> Bank through the Deep and Comprehensive Free Trade Area (DCFTA) facility, targeting SMEs and supporting investments in energy efficiency.
>
> - The European Investment Bank (EIB) has supported a number of banks through integrated SME and environment loans. EIB has provided EUR 165 million for SMEs through three Georgian banks (BoG, TBC Bank, ProCredit Bank). The EIB Group also provides partial portfolio credit guarantees under the EU Finance for Innovators (InnovFin)[5] and DCFTA programmes, so far to TBC Bank and ProCredit Bank. EIB has also supported the microfinance sector that provides microlending to small and micro businesses in Georgia (Credo Bank).
>
> - KfW provided a EUR 25 million loan to BoG. It was supported by a EUR 0.75 million technical assistance package, with a risk-sharing facility supported by OeEB in 2012. The facility, with a maturity of ten years, is mainly used to provide long-term loan finance for the construction or rehabilitation of small-sized hydropower plants up to 20 megawatts.
>
> - OeEB provided ProCredit Bank with a USD 15 million credit line for SME energy efficiency in 2012. OeEB also supports a range of relevant technical advisory and risk-sharing facilities in the Caucasus. These include financing the National Cleaner Production Center in Georgia, set up by the United Nations Industrial Development Organization and the United Nations Environment Programme. They also include a risk facility supporting a KfW loan supporting small hydropower development through BoG.
>
> - Green for Growth Fund provided a USD 15 million credit line to BoG for energy-efficient housing in 2014. It provided a USD 15 million credit line to TBC Bank in 2015 for renewable energy (RE)/EE lending activities. Finally, it provided a USD 5 million credit line to Bank Republic (TBC Bank since 2016) for green lending to households.
>
> - GCPF provided a USD 25 million debt facility to TBC Bank to support renewable energy development in Georgia in 2017.
>
> *Source:* Various fund websites and personal communication with staff of the banks.

Table 4.1 sets out Georgian banks that have received IFI-supported credit lines since 2008.

Table 4.1. Overview of Georgia's financial institutions receiving IFI support

	EBRD	EIB	FMO	GCPF	GGF	KfW	OeEB
Bank of Georgia	X	X			X	X	Xa
Bank Republic	X	X			X		
Basis Bank	X						
Credo Bank	X	X					
Crystal Microfinance				X			
ProCredit Bank		X					
TBC Bank	X	X	X	X	X	X	X
VTB Bank	X						

Notes: FMO = Dutch Entrepreneurial Development Bank; GCPF = Global Climate Partnership Fund; GGF = Green for Growth Fund; KfW = Kreditanstalt für Wiederaufbau; OeEB = Development Bank of Austria.
X[a] - Unfunded risk-sharing facility alongside a KfW loan.
Source: Authors' review of IFI/fund reports.

Microfinance institutions, institutional investors and non-financial sector corporations play a limited role in financial flows for climate action in Georgia. Some microfinance organisations, such as MFO Crystal, are making progress in designing and providing loans to energy-efficiency activities and smaller-scale, often decentralised, renewable energy facilities. The same is true for commercial banks that primarily target SMEs, such as JSC ProCredit Bank. The Dutch Entrepreneurial Development Bank (FMO) started to work with MFO Crystal on a green microfinance programme in 2017.

There have also been examples of domestic equity investments. For example, the government-owned JSC Partnership Fund made equity investments in the production of green construction materials in 2016. However, these investments tend to be oriented towards medium and large companies or platforms. Georgia also participates in the Global Energy Efficiency and Renewable Energy Fund programme, which finances private equity investors making green investments.

4.4. Local banks that provide green finance in Georgia

This subsection sets out the experience of the three most active banks in providing green finance in Georgia – BoG, ProCredit Bank Georgia and TBC Bank (in alphabetical order). All three offer a mixture of SME and corporate lending products depending on the size of client. All three have also participated in IFI green credit lines. However, each has taken a different approach to SME green finance.

- *BoG*, one of the two leading banks in Georgia, operates a broad spectrum of services. The bank services 2.5 million clients through a network of 271 retail branches and has approximately a 35% market share in terms of total assets, loans and customer deposits. It operates a multi-brand strategy in retail banking, which consists of emerging and mass retail (Express and flagship branches, express pay-terminals, mobile and internet banking), Solo (banking products and services for more affluent segments), and micro/SME segment. It also provides banking services to its corporate clients. BoG is the leading corporate lender in Georgia, servicing more than 2 500 businesses across a range of sectors, including trade, energy industry and tourism. It also serves as the country's leading trade finance business and provides leasing services through its wholly-owned subsidiary, Georgian Leasing Company. The bank is the core entity of Bank of Georgia Group PLC (the Group), listed company on the premium segment of the London Stock Exchange's main market for listed securities, which is a constituent of the Financial Times and Stock Exchange (FTSE) 250 Index. The Group also provides a range of services through corporate advisory, debt and equity capital, market research and brokerage practices under its wholly-owned subsidiary Galt and Taggart. BoG has been a leading proponent of green lending in the Georgian market. It has taken multiple credit lines with IFIs to promote energy efficiency and renewable energy lending (EBRD, EIB, KfW and GGF).

- *TBC Bank* is a universal bank operating in Georgia that serves retail, SME and corporate clients. In 2016, TBC Bank purchased Bank Republic from Societe Generale, making it the largest Georgian bank in terms of loans and deposits. Its share of total loans reached nearly 38% and its share of non-banking deposits reached nearly 39% at the beginning of 2018, according to the National Bank of Georgia. It has more than 2 million clients and 170 branches across Georgia. TBC Bank is listed on the London Stock Exchange and is a constituent of the FTSE 250 index. It has received a number of credit lines from five IFIs to promote energy efficiency and renewable energy investments, as well as to support green growth for corporates and SMEs.

- *ProCredit Bank Georgia* has been operating in the Georgian banking sector since 1999. Its core aim is to finance SMEs alongside retail clients. ProCredit Bank Georgia is part of the international ProCredit group of banks operating mainly in Eastern and South East Europe, as well as in Germany. ProCredit Holding, the parent company, serves the SME business sector, offering comprehensive banking services based on the German "Hausbank" principle. The ProCredit group is listed on the Frankfurt Stock Exchange's Prime Standard. The Co-finance Programme between ProCredit Bank Georgia and ProCredit Bank Germany allows Georgian SMEs with larger financing requirements (EUR 750 000–5 million) to be financed at preferential interest rates. ProCredit has a strong social and environmental policy, with an environmental management system. It was the first bank in Georgia to obtain ISO 14001 certification. ProCredit Bank offers Eco Loans to support investments in energy-efficient materials and equipment supporting both SMEs and households to improve productivity and efficiency. Retail loans are offered for housing upgrade and electric transport transition, but are not branded explicitly as eco-loans. The Bank's green lending constitutes 16% of its total loan portfolio.

All three banks benefit from access to international capital markets and well-developed governance models (either through their main shareholder or as a result of listing on established stock exchanges).

4.5. Key success factors

All three banks share several differentiating features that have enabled them to successfully participate in providing green credit to the SME sector. Senior management and staff identified the following common key reasons for their success:

- *Senior management buy-in and support:* All the banks demonstrate strategic support at senior management level for engagement in the environmental finance market with a clear view of the benefits this can bring for market share and profitability. They also engaged early with IFI lending programmes to support energy efficiency and renewable energy on-lending. Together with strong commitment to international governance standards and environmental and social mandate, this early engagement allowed all three banks to build strong reputations and skills in the marketplace.

- *Standard bank product development:* All three banks have sought to align support from international IFIs and donors into standard products aligned with their core client base. Where each IFI has different lending and reporting criteria, these tend to be blended from a front-end perspective – with the concessionality and tenor blended and packaged for clients. This has allowed the banks to take full product ownership, rather than just act as an intermediary for individual IFI lending operations.

- *Dedicated in-house capacity:* All three banks have dedicated significant internal resources to developing and promoting energy efficiency and renewable energy lending products on the Georgian market. This has included building capacity in loan appraisal (e.g. the incorporation of energy savings into cash-flow and payback analysis). It has also included renewable energy product finance; marketing; training for branch staff in promoting products; and environmental reporting (e.g. energy savings, GHG emission calculations).

- *Economies of scale:* All three banks, as the leading financial institutions in Georgia, have a well-established client base. This has provided them with a strong and diversified pipeline of customers for energy efficiency and renewable energy finance products. The client profile is highly diversified from a sector profile. The banks have been able to achieve economies of scale in product development and distribution. All three have strong marketing capacity to promote the product using client success stories. All three also have international share capital that has allowed them to maintain a level of financial robustness during periods of political and economic stability.

- *Ability to work with international donors*: All three banks enjoy strong corporate governance regimes and international shareholder base. This has facilitated co-operation with IFIs, which often struggle to engage with banks that present reputational risk.

4.6. Key challenges

There is a lack of affordable long-term capital for smaller-scale SMEs in Georgia. This can severely impact their ability to make investments in clean energy, energy efficiency and other sustainability improvements. Discussions with representatives of the three banks identified several challenges that prevent the scale up of green finance to the SME market in Georgia. These are outlined below.

Supply side

- *Definition of SMEs and large average loan size*: Georgian banks co-operating with IFIs to disburse green credit lines use international standards for defining and reporting on the eligibility of borrowers (see earlier discussions on SME definitions). As a result, funds have tended to flow to larger companies, often classified as corporates in the Georgian context (although classified as SMEs under EU standards). For this reason, the average SME loan size for energy efficiency has been relatively large (often in excess of USD 1 million) for BoG and TBC Bank. Further, much of the loan business has originated through their corporate banking departments rather than through their SME departments. The same is true for ProCredit Bank. The size of its SME loan under the Eco-Loan programme at EUR 750 000–5 million is significantly larger than what smaller businesses might require. It is attractive for banks to issue smaller numbers of larger loans as this reduces transaction costs. This, in turn, allows the banks to target more creditworthy customers and increases their potential return on capital.

- *A tendency to direct green finance towards hydropower development:* Some of the early green credit lines negotiated with IFIs (e.g. EBRD's Energocredit facility) were structured to be interchangeable across renewable energy and energy efficiency. This reflected concerns over the lack of demand for energy-efficiency borrowing at sufficient scale to allow for credit-line disbursement according to envisaged timescales. As a result, significant funds were used for hydropower projects rather than SME lending. Hydropower in Georgia has attracted significant private investor interest (both domestic and international). Moreover, local banks in Georgia have developed strong capacity in evaluating and investing in such projects. These projects became attractive due to the availability of power purchase agreements and other policy support.

- *Opportunity costs for banks:* Banks are often faced with opportunity costs when deciding whether to actively promote green lending products to the SME sector. When lending to SMEs, banks often have a range of more "straightforward" and shorter-term products (e.g. standard SME finance) that can provide good returns and for which there is a growing market. Banks can also choose instead to target other larger and more profitable segments through their branch networks (e.g. mortgage finance, retail banking). There are opportunity costs for investing in what are perceived to be green lending products with a potentially smaller customer base and higher transaction costs. This is especially the case where there are more stringent eligibility and reporting requirements. Often, particularly when co-operating with IFI credit lines, significant transaction costs are associated with SME green lending. These could include more complex loan applications, energy audits, feasibility studies, monitoring and reporting of results. These can make such loans less profitable or require higher pricing. It remains to be seen how many of the banks that have co-operated with IFIs will continue to offer green lending products once their credit lines are disbursed.

- *Insufficient capacity for appraising green projects in banks:* Banks have been relatively slow to understand the green lending market. The use of minimum energy-saving criteria can mean that cash-flow and project-finance analysis should be used alongside more mainstream standard credit assessment procedures. The use of project finance is still relatively rare in the SME space in Georgia (and elsewhere). Lending decisions are usually based on standard credit decision criteria. Banks are also initially risk averse as they lack familiarity with the green technologies and processes being financed. They may also be unaware of what types of projects within their wider lending portfolio may be suitable for green finance. Banks may also prefer to fund projects that increase capacity and productivity (where potential returns are clear) rather than those that simply reduce costs. Energy-efficiency projects often have rapid payback periods [see (OeEB, 2015[8])]. However, the short tenor and high cost of finance in Georgia make the prospect of resource efficiency less attractive than it might otherwise be.

- *Constraints around equity investment:* Public and private sector investors have provided equity investments, particularly to larger-scale renewable energy and hydropower projects. However, equity is much less available for smaller-scale, non-hydro renewables and energy-efficiency projects. Capital markets are underdeveloped in Georgia. As a result, SMEs looking to scale their operations into sustainable development sectors lack access to angel investors, venture capital or private equity investors.

Demand side

- *Lack of awareness among borrowers:* There is a lack of awareness among potential borrowers (particularly smaller SMEs) of the potential benefits accruing from investments in energy-efficiency projects. This is combined with exaggerated perceptions of risk associated with technology and financing. Borrowers do not view their capital investment programmes specifically in terms of energy efficiency or climate change benefits. Often, those making investment decisions are unaware of the real payback periods associated with such investments. They may have a poor understanding of the co-benefits in terms of improved quality and productivity. Investment in green technologies or energy efficiency for SMEs may often be regarded as an opportunity cost at the expense of increasing production or developing new products. SMEs may not know about the full range of best practices that can be integrated alongside capital investment and how they can also improve financial returns on projects.

- *Incomplete strategic and regulatory frameworks* continue to limit demand for sustainable energy finance. The incremental development, adoption and implementation of national energy-efficiency policies and associated sub-regulations serve to constrain the potential market for sustainable energy finance. Ongoing energy subsidies for fossil fuels also distort investment decisions, although recent pricing reform is now beginning to drive demand. An OECD study on energy subsidies in the EU Eastern Partnership countries shows that in the natural gas sector in Georgia, consumption is significantly subsidised, for the needs of both electricity generation and distribution for heating and cooking. Natural gas subsidies come in the form of regulated tariffs, value-added tax exemption and direct budget transfers (OECD, 2018[9]).

> **Box 4.2. Examples of criteria for ProCredit Bank eco loans**
>
> ProCredit Bank offers eco loans for SMEs to address a range of efficiency upgrades and renewable investments. Examples of qualifying investments include the following:
>
> - Production processes – replacing old machines or equipment or purchasing additional machines or equipment
> - Building envelope – applying thermal insulation to external walls/ceilings/floors and installing double-/triple-glazed windows or doors
> - Electrical equipment – purchasing high-efficiency electric motors, new lighting systems, appliances rated A+ and above, etc.
> - Heating or cooling – installing new central heating/cooling systems, boilers, air conditioners, etc.
> - Waste management – separation of waste, recycling (paper, plastic, glass) prevention of waste, etc.
> - Renewable energy sources – installing solar water heating systems (flat collectors, vacuum tube collectors), ground heat pumps or biomass boilers (wood, pellet, etc.).
>
> *Source*: ProCredit Bank.

4.7. Policy response

Providing smaller-scale SMEs with improved access to finance for green investment has been difficult. The government has been exploring this challenge during the development of recent climate-related development frameworks.

Both the Low Emission Development Strategy (LEDS) and the draft National Energy Efficiency Action Plan (NEEAP) stress the need for funding mechanisms to support the scale up of green finance. These would be supported by a broader national focus on investment promotion and facilitation and financial market development (although not necessarily focused on SMEs).

NEEAP has proposed a dedicated agency[6] that would seek to scale green investment. It would target such areas as green infrastructure, energy efficiency and potentially renewable energy (OECD, 2018[10]). Such an agency would have the following qualities:

- be managed as an independent agency outside of the ministry structure
- have a longer-term financing period (e.g. two-three years) for more strategic planning
- support donor co-ordination
- facilitate blended finance to support other public and private sector investment
- be capitalised from budgetary resources

- be supported over time through other revenue streams (e.g. energy bills; taxes on inefficient goods and services such as vehicles; and environmental fines).

LEDS has also explored a range of options for mobilising green finance, including the following:

- developing a climate finance strategy roadmap
- establishing a national green investment bank
- creating a climate finance task force to improve budgeting, planning and analysis
- improving the use of blended finance
- exploring bond finance for climate-related projects.

Any funds (whether a national investment bank or other financing platform) must clearly be able to work alongside platforms to achieve the reach and distribution to address SME financing challenges. One option would be to partner with Enterprise Georgia and the commercial banking sector (see Annex A). Such an approach could incorporate green criteria into their existing concessional support for SMEs in the "Produce in Georgia" Programme.

Notes

[1] Information provided by EBRD during the Policy Dialogue meeting in Tbilisi in July 2019.

[2] The EU taxonomy is a tool to help investors understand whether an economic activity is environmentally sustainable. The EU taxonomy contains (i) technical screening criteria for 67 activities across 8 sectors that can make a substantial contribution to climate change mitigation; (ii) a methodology and worked examples for evaluating substantial contribution to climate change adaptation; (iii) guidance and case studies for investors preparing to use the taxonomy.

[3] Discussions with Georgian commercial banks indicate that green loans are normally priced in a way similar to other types of SME lending.

[4] Marginal abatement costs can be negative when the low-carbon option is cheaper than the business-as-usual option. However, marginal abatement costs can often rise steeply as more pollution is reduced.

[5] The InnovFin SME Guarantee scheme aims to facilitate and accelerate access to loan finance for innovative SME businesses and provides guarantees on debt financing between EUR 25 000 and EUR 7.5 million.

[6] This agency is envisaged to function more like a supervisory board that will be tasked to oversee energy efficiency issues in the country. The government of Georgia is reconsidering establishment of such an agency but final solution is still pending.

References

EBRD/World Bank Group (2015), *The Business Environment in the Transition Region (based on the Business Environment and Enterprise Performance Survey)*, European Bank for Reconstruction and Development, London; World Bank Group, Washington, DC, https://ebrd-beeps.com/wp-content/uploads/2015/07/BEEPSV-complete.pdf. [6]

Government of Georgia (2015), *Georgia's Intended Nationally Determined Contribution*, United Nations Framework Convention on Climate Change, Bonn, http://www4.unfccc.int/submissions/INDC/Published%20Documents/Georgia/1/INDC_of_Georgia.pdf. [4]

Government of Georgia (2015), *Third National Communication of Georgia to the UN Framework Convention on Climate Change*, United Nations Development Programme, Tbilisi, https://www.ge.undp.org/content/georgia/en/home/library/environment_energy/third-national-communication-of-georgia-to-the-un-framework-conv0/. [3]

NBG (2019), *Key Macroeconomic Indicators and International Ratings*, National Bank of Georgia (database) (accessed 23 October 2019), https://www.nbg.gov.ge/index.php?m=494&lng=eng. [5]

NEEAP Expert Team (2017), *Draft National Energy Efficiency Action Plan, Report Commissioned by EBRD*, National Energy Efficiency Action Plan, Tbilisi. [1]

OECD (2018), *Inventory of Energy Subsidies in the EU's Eastern Partnership Countries*, Green Finance and Investment, OECD Publishing, Paris, http://www.oecd.org/env/inventory-of-energy-subsidies-in-the-eu-s-eastern-partnership-countries-9789264284319-en.htm. [9]

OECD (2018), *Mobilising Finance for Climate Action in Georgia*, Green Finance and Investment, OECD Publishing, Paris, https://dx.doi.org/10.1787/9789264289727-en. [10]

OECD (2016), *Environmental Lending in EU Eastern Partnership Countries*, Green Finance and Investment, OECD Publishing, Paris, https://dx.doi.org/10.1787/9789264252189-en. [7]

OeEB (2015), *Energy Efficiency Potential. Final Country Report: Georgia, Energy Efficiency Finance II TASK 1*, Development Bank of Austria, Vienna, https://www.oe-eb.at/dam/jcr:c480882f-df26-4d62-9901-d6e25e2a4ec1/OeEB-Study-Energy-Efficiency-Finance-Georgia.pdf. [8]

Winrock and Remissia (2017), *Georgia Low Emission Development Strategy Draft Report*, commissioned by the USAID-funded EC-LEDS Clean Energy Program, Winrock International and Sustainable Development Center, Little Rock, US. [2]

Chapter 5. Recommendations for policy makers

The chapter summarises the main conclusions and findings that have emerged from the analysis. It also offers recommendations targeted at policy makers in the government of Georgia. Among other concerns, these touch upon improvements in the macroeconomic situation and investment climate, political and institutional environment, and access to and cost of finance. These include barriers related to issues such as the policy and regulatory environment; the cost of, and access to, finance; energy pricing; and fossil-fuel subsidies.

Local financial institutions in Georgia have sought to strengthen sustainable energy markets by developing lending products to promote energy efficiency. Banks have also provided debt finance to developers of small hydro projects. This has helped the Georgian economy move towards a more sustainable and competitive development pathway. It also reflects the government's push towards a more resource-efficient, low-carbon economy.

International financial institutions (IFIs) have provided significant volumes of sustainable energy credit-line facilities to at least eight commercial Georgian banks and financial institutions. These credit lines have been used to provide on-lending to industry, commercial companies and households, primarily for investment in energy efficiency.

The market for energy-efficiency investments is likely to be significantly larger than that represented by these facilities. Much of the investment is in energy efficiency served by mainstream corporate and small and medium-sized enterprise (SME) lending products. However, there are no explicit requirements in their loans to recognise energy savings and associated impacts of greenhouse gas (GHG) mitigation.

Promoting energy efficiency among SMEs has a range of benefits at the national level. For example, it can address competitiveness challenges by reducing the high costs of fossil-fuel inputs. It can also improve energy security by reducing dependence on imports of fossil fuel. However, Georgian policy makers have not typically viewed the area of sustainable energy lending, particularly to SME borrowers, as an area for direct government engagement or support.

Green lending is usually regarded as a fully commercial transaction between private institutions. Such investments are generally undertaken primarily for their productivity and cost benefits. Environmental or other co-benefits are usually an afterthought, if they are considered at all. Both government and IFIs assume that market dynamics for energy-efficiency finance would be self-supporting once the model had been demonstrated and borrowers could show net savings. Yet the market for green finance in Georgia has not developed as quickly as expected.

This report outlines several barriers that continue to hold back the development of a dynamic market. These include a policy and regulatory environment that remains "work-in-progress", issues of cost of and access to finance, perverse incentives associated with energy pricing and fossil-fuel subsidies, and wider investment climate issues in Georgia. Policy makers can play a key enabling role to overcome many of these barriers, which are described in more detail below.

5.1. Strengthen environmental policy and regulation

A range of policy reforms is already promoting sustainable energy, climate and environmental performance, and wider green growth. However, significant work remains to finalise the laws and regulations that can underpin demand for green finance, particularly in relation to SMEs. Further details are set out below:

- *Strengthen environmental legislation:* Legislation associated with the Third Energy Package and other European Union (EU) directives, together with laws associated with the Energy Community, need to be finalised and fully adopted. However, while primary legislation is important, it is not enough. The government must support technical implementation by developing effective sub-regulations and supporting programmes. Ambitious energy-efficiency standards for energy-consuming appliances, transport and buildings need to be enforced and ratcheted upwards over time. Other areas of technical support include raising awareness of energy efficiency among end-user groups, promoting energy management systems (e.g. ISO 50 000 series standards, International Performance Measurement and Verification Protocol) and audits as part of energy services provision. The government might also consider developing a clean energy industrial strategy to promote indigenous technology and services provision.

- *Ensure alignment of SME, climate and relevant sector policies:* As noted earlier, Georgia has a growing and increasingly complex framework (policies, strategies and implementing programmes) for both green growth and SME development. The government needs to ensure consistency and integration between its policies and targets for renewable energy, energy-efficiency and GHG emission reductions. It also needs to ensure these objectives are aligned with, and reflected in, wider development objectives and sector programmes, particularly where these support SMEs.

- *Strengthen environmental regulation and enforcement:* Weak environmental regulation and enforcement (e.g. around emissions, waste, pollution, buildings, transport) can reduce the incentive for SMEs to focus on environmental performance and reduce demand for finance. Georgian enterprises, from small- to large-scale, consider stricter environmental policies and better enforcement to be the most important lever to influence investment decisions. Such decisions could revolve, for example, around resource-efficiency and cleaner-production measures (OECD, 2018[1]).

- *Develop tax and other incentive frameworks*: The Ministry of Economy and Sustainable Development (MESD) should discuss further tax incentives for environmental investments with the Ministry of Finance. These include accelerated amortisation and reduced taxes for renewable energy and energy-efficiency equipment, and possibly a corporate-tax credit for environmental investments.

- *Promote green procurement through SMEs.* Government spending on goods and services accounts for 18.4% of Georgian gross domestic product (World Bank, 2017[2]). In fact, Georgia's State Procurement Agency has already considered integrating environmental and energy performance criteria into the Law on Public Procurement. The government should also review the ability of SMEs to engage with the procurement system. This process should ensure that SMEs can better enter the competitive market for the provision of sustainable goods and services (OECD, 2016[3]), (Singh, 2016[4]).

- *Rationalise energy pricing:* Relatively low energy prices in Georgia are positive for economic development. However, they have limited the incentive for SME investment in resource and energy efficiency and small-scale decentralised renewables. The government amended the Tax Code in 2017 to increase tax rates on fossil fuels. Natural gas, however, is still subsidised for electricity and heat generation, albeit at a lower level than some other countries in the region. The government should continue to pursue reforms to energy pricing. This includes integrating social protection for the poorest and most vulnerable energy consumers into energy tariff structures. Additional social protection measures based on income should be introduced through the welfare system. This would help avoid confusing and perverse price signals in relation to energy use.

5.2. Define role of SMEs in the green transition

In designing energy and sustainable development strategy, policy makers often focus on the role of larger companies and banks in financing and implementation. Policy makers should consider more explicitly the role of SMEs in delivering national targets. These targets should include those related to both energy efficiency and wider resource efficiency:

- *Better consideration of SMEs in the development of green financing frameworks:* It is not clear to what extent smaller SMEs have been considered during development of the National Energy Efficiency Action Plan (NEEAP) and the Low Emission Development Strategy (LEDS). Their concerns and challenges should be considered more closely during future policy development. This could include, for example, revisions of the NEEAP and LEDS, and development of the Green Economy Strategy or of the Intended Nationally Determined Contribution (INDC). This will allow a level of co-ordination and coherence in policy development.

- *Understanding the role of SMEs in delivering national policies and targets:* Georgia is committed to delivering its climate and sustainable development goals through a range of public and private strategies. At a sub-national level, these include the Municipal Project Support Facility, European Bank for Reconstruction and Development's Green City Framework and the Asian Development Bank's Tbilisi Sustainable Urban Transport Programme. For these types of programmes, SMEs and their participation should be an explicit consideration.

- *Better estimates of SME financing requirements as part of the green transition:* More robust estimates are required that downscale the national estimates of climate finance set out in the NEEAP, LEDS and INDC. These would show what percentage of finance is likely to be required by public vs. private actors, and by SMEs. This would be particularly important for priority thematic areas such as energy efficiency, buildings upgrade and small-scale renewable energy.

5.3. Improve wider access to finance for SMEs

Green investment cannot occur while Georgian SMEs experience wider challenges in accessing finance. To benefit from new export opportunities offered by the Deep and Comprehensive Free Trade Area arrangement, Georgian SMEs will need to invest in and modernise their businesses to improve competitiveness. The recommendations for the SME development strategy include five priority actions: (i) amend the legal framework on public grants; (ii) improve supply-side financial skills to leverage the regional presence of banks; (iii) promote demand-side financial education programmes targeting SME entrepreneurs; (iv) consider establishing a credit guarantee scheme as a risk-sharing mechanism; and (v) improve alternative non-bank and equity financing for SMEs.

- *Amend the legal framework on public grants:* Georgia needs to amend the laws regulating the provision of public grants. Amending the Law on Grants (PoG, 1996) is a prerequisite for the design of effective SME support policies implemented by Georgian Enterprise Development Agency (EDA/Enterprise Georgia), Georgia's Innovation and Technology Agency (GITA) and other institutions that aim at providing financial assistance to companies struggling to access bank lending in Georgia.

- *Improve SME banking capacity:* Georgia should improve the capacity of its banking sector to serve SMEs better. The government could partner with key stakeholders such as the National Bank of Georgia and the Association of Banks of Georgia to develop country-wide capacity-building programmes for SME banking. This could be done through certification programmes by including topics such as products and delivery channels for SMEs. In addition, risk management courses could help identify the fundamental causes of SME risks and the tools required to manage them. Credit scores, for example, could assess borrowers' creditworthiness. Further, forums for the managers of banks' SME departments could be organised to share international best practice in the field.

- *Promote demand-side financial education programmes targeting SME entrepreneurs.* Georgia could put in place financial education initiatives to improve entrepreneurs' financial skills. This would help reduce the asymmetry of information between SMEs and potential lenders, and thus the risk perceived by the latter. SMEs need greater knowledge of the financial products available in the market, as well as how to produce credible business plans and sound financial statements for loan applications. Enterprise Georgia has taken some positive steps already. These include creating a library of financial training materials, an SME toolkit and "mini-Master of Business Administration" courses for beneficiaries of "Produce in Georgia". Further support could be organised through regional Chambers of Commerce and possibly with the participation of the National Bank of Georgia and the Association of Banks.

- *Expand credit guarantee schemes*: The Georgian government recently introduced a new credit guarantee scheme (CGS) to promote SMEs' financial inclusion and address difficult collateral requirements. The budget for this scheme is rather modest but this is a first phase only and the scheme can be further adjusted and expanded. A CGS works as a risk-sharing mechanism between lenders (banks), borrowers (SMEs) and a guarantor (the state or a private entity). A CGS effectively creates market-based incentives for banks to lend more to SMEs. By reducing the perceived risk, banks are expected to request lower collateral and interest rates from borrowing SMEs. As a result, more credit is extended to borrowers than otherwise would be the case in the absence of a CGS.

- *Improve alternative non-bank and equity financing for SMEs.* The venture capital environment in Georgia could be further strengthened to foster improved access to capital for small and dynamic growing businesses. A fund could be established to act as a catalyst for private capital and to match early investment in SMEs with high-growth potential. The government could devise schemes to promote venture capital and early stage investment in Georgian SMEs. Such schemes would ensure economic additionality in the early stages of the funds. Public sector involvement could phase out as private markets mature. The government could also promote alternative forms of asset-based financing. These could include leasing and factoring (i.e. the sale of accounts receivable to a third party). In addition, it could promote awareness of investment opportunities, and support establishment of a network of business angels to provide expertise and capital through dedicated events.

5.4. Improve the availability and terms of green finance for SMEs

SMEs continue to face significant barriers when seeking access to green finance. Issues include the level of interest rates, the tenor and collateral requirements. Several options could improve the availability of green finance, and the terms on which SMEs can access it.

- *Exploring new green financing instruments:* Georgia should explore the role of dedicated concessional green instruments/funds to help widen access and improve the terms of environmental finance for SMEs. Building on ideas in both LEDS and NEEAP, such funds could provide direct green investment in projects (e.g. as partial grant co-finance for underserved market segments). Alternatively, they could offer green credit enhancement, such as blended finance with lower rates and longer tenor. They might also offer risk mitigation instruments for green lending portfolios, such as first loss and partial credit guarantees. This could be provided to existing commercial banks, as well as microfinance institutions by third parties, to widen access.

- *Expanding green finance distribution channels for smaller SMEs:* Smaller SMEs struggle to access IFI-supported green finance credit. The government could consider promoting green finance through other channels (e.g. microfinance organisations). Such channels have good distribution networks, but the cost of finance is high and tenors are short. Preferential leasing terms for green/energy efficient equipment and energy service company models might also help overcome collateral and capital barriers faced by smaller SMEs.

- *Promoting concessionality:* While IFIs are committed to not distorting commercial lending markets for energy-efficiency and renewable-energy lending, the cost of finance remains an issue. IFIs should consider encouraging differential pricing for green lending facilities, encouraging pass through of interest rate benefits to end borrowers. Where possible, IFIs should encourage development of local currency-lending facilities for green investment to reduce currency exposure for SME investment in energy efficiency and renewable energy.

- *Using existing institutional structures to channel funding to SMEs*: The role of state funds or entities could be expanded to incorporate a green mandate. Such structures would need to facilitate access to smaller-scale SMEs. This could occur either through their own programmes or platforms, or through a partnership with local financial institutions to reduce transaction costs. Potential structures might include the JSC Partnership Fund, the JSC Georgian Energy Development Fund or Enterprise Georgia. The first two of these, however, might lack the scale and scope to support redirecting financial flows towards climate and green growth agendas. This is especially the case in underserved sectors or companies such as SMEs. The government should base its decision on a review of relevant structures. To that end, it should assess whether any given national funding entities could aggregate large numbers of smaller projects to reduce risk, lower transaction costs and potentially gain access to international capital.

- *Exploring the role of Enterprise Georgia:* Enterprise Georgia provides perhaps the most useful vehicle to support the scale up of green investment in Georgia. It has an established network and platform to engage with smaller-scale companies across the country. The MESD and Enterprise Georgia could work with local financing institutions to incorporate cleaner production and resource-efficiency considerations into conditions of financial support for SMEs. Banks could also be encouraged to use environmental criteria in their credit decisions. The MESD and Enterprise Georgia should consider providing grants to SMEs. These would cover part of consultancy/audit costs to identify and implement resource efficiency, an environmental management system or other environmentally oriented measures. Such grants should be offered through a competitive application process and cover no more than half of total costs.

5.5. Scale the overall availability of green finance in the Georgian economy

As part of delivering Georgia's sustainable development strategy, a significant step-change in both public and private sector green investment will be required to support SMEs. The government of Georgia should therefore examine how it might work with partners and domestic financial institutions to achieve a step-change in the wider availability of environmental finance.

- *Exploring green banking regulation:* The government of Georgia should continue to review and develop green banking regulations to improve sustainable lending and asset management among local financial institutions. This can be done in several ways. Better frameworks could identify and classify "green" and "brown" assets using, for example, the work carried out under the European Union Taxonomy on Sustainable Activities. Better reporting and disclosure could help disclose high carbon assets and or climate risk. Over the long term, the government could also consider preferential treatment of green assets through, for example, differentiated capital reserve requirements. The recent NBG "Roadmap for Sustainable Finance" (NBG, 2019[5]) represents a step in this direction. The Roadmap and the Action Plan until 2022 envisage several measures. These include introduction of a sustainable finance taxonomy, and integrating environmental, social and governance considerations into the relevant corporate governance codes for commercial banks and the capital market. These measures will need to be translated into practical guidance and support tools. They can be expected to green the financial market and improve its transparency and market discipline.

- *Considering the issuance of green bonds:* Georgia could support the development of a green bond market, with potential benefits for SME development. Government (with IFI support) could issue green bonds and encourage long-term domestic and international investors (e.g. pension funds) to invest. This could raise funds for green projects and potentially with dedicated windows for the SME sector. The government of Georgia and the National Bank of Georgia would have to develop green bond standards or adopt those used in other countries.

- *Pooling international and domestic capital:* At a macro level, the government should consider working to pool national and international climate and environmental funds. These would create financing and technical implementation platforms that can be transformational in their size and scope. This is particularly important when addressing sectors such as SME finance. In these sectors, economies of scale are difficult to achieve, significant structural barriers exist and borrower creditworthiness is a concern. Sources of initial capitalisation are likely to include donor funds, the Green Climate Fund and other forms of development finance for investment in energy-efficiency projects. These may be one approach to capitalisation.

- *Exploring a possible role for a national development bank or fund:* The government may wish to consider creating a new bank or national fund to support the distribution of finance. National development banks are often used to achieve developmental policy aims through concessional funds. Such institutions should be careful not to distort markets for commercial players (e.g. by picking winners or crowding out commercial banks). They also need to ensure appropriate levels of concessions and subsidies so that beneficiaries are not overcompensated. Such a fund would also need to build capacity to undertake project appraisal, monitor projects and evaluation results. In addition, it should help support market development with better data and insight into the benefits of green investment.

5.6. Raise awareness among SMEs of green transition opportunities

- *Raising awareness of green opportunities among SMEs*: SMEs often have a poorer understanding of available opportunities compared to larger, better-resourced companies. Better understanding among potential borrowers about energy-efficiency technologies and their cost-benefit profiles could improve demand for green investment. Countries are also setting up learning networks and platforms to improve information flows, raise awareness of benefits from green investment and good national and international practices, and enhance analytical capabilities.

- *Supporting development of tools and methods to assist SME environmental performance:* The government could create programmes to support the development of (and access to) environmental performance and management tools targeted at SMEs. These might initially be focused around energy management. They could include simple calculators to help understand the payback potential for improved efficiency, as well as to advise on how to access further support and finance.

- *Strengthen "green branding":* Strong environmental and social performance is increasingly a key element for branding and market positioning. In some SME-relevant sectors (e.g. hotels, transport), sustainability is becoming a key differentiator, with energy and wider resource efficiency as a core component. The government could seek to identify SME sectors where environmental performance is a brand driver. It could then work with these sectors to promote uptake of more environmental technologies, including supporting national and international certification schemes.

References

NBG (2019), "Roadmap for Sustainable Finance in Georgia", National Bank of Georgia, webpage (accessed 23 October 2019), https://www.nbg.gov.ge/uploads/finstability/roadmap/sustainable_finance_roadmap_eng.pdf. [5]

OECD (2018), *Mobilising Finance for Climate Action in Georgia*, Green Finance and Investment, OECD Publishing, Paris, https://dx.doi.org/10.1787/9789264289727-en. [1]

OECD (2016), *Promoting Better Environmental Performance of SMEs: Georgia*, OECD Publishing, Paris, http://www.oecd.org/env/outreach/Georgia%20pilot%20project%20report%20final%20EN.pdf. [3]

Singh, J. (2016), *Energy Efficiency Financing Option Papers for Georgia*, World Bank, Washington, DC, http://documents.worldbank.org/curated/en/825761475845097689/Energy-efficiency-financing-option-papers-for-Georgia. [4]

World Bank (2017), *Georgia – Private Sector Competitiveness Development Policy Operation*, World Bank, Washington, DC, http://documents.worldbank.org/curated/en/478801501725663367/pdf/Georgia-Private-Sector-Competitiveness-PD-07112017.pdf. [2]

Annex A. Georgia's banking sector

Annex A provides some basic information on the role and capacity of the banking sector in Georgia to support the economic development of the country. It also looks at the main trends in the banking sector, particularly since the last financial crisis. The annex introduces major reforms that the government of Georgia could consider. These reforms would aim to create an effective and competitive banking system that can also offer higher volumes of green lending.

Market structure and concentration

There is a high degree of concentration in the Georgian banking sector. The top three banks account for 79% of assets with the top two, TBC Bank and Bank of Georgia (BoG), accounting for 74% of assets.

The Georgian financial sector is almost entirely dependent on banks (90%+). Capital markets remain underdeveloped, potentially due to structural issues. The equity market is highly illiquid. Sovereign bonds are liquid, but private bond issuance is limited.

Figure A A.1. Non-banking financial assets as a share of total assets, 2008-18

Source: (NBG, 2019[1]).

In 2017, the International Finance Corporation supported the BoG in its first local currency Eurobond issuance. It invested about USD 45 million helping to attract about USD 250 million from about 20 international investors. This three-year bond was the first in the past decade from a country in the European Union's Eastern Partnership (EaP) region other than the Russian Federation. It supported local-currency lending and de-dollarisation efforts. The issuance allowed the bank to boost long-term local-currency financing to more retail borrowers, and small and medium-sized enterprises (SMEs). This aims to help them avoid risks related to borrowing in foreign currency (Agenda.GE, 2017[2]).

However, policy makers need to take certain precautions. For example, they must ensure open entry to the market and competition. They must also ensure that sufficiently strong safeguards are in place to prevent collusion or market dominance. Finally, they must ensure that the two institutions, Bank of Georgia (BoG) and TBC Bank, do not become "too big to fail".

Georgia has a relatively weak legislative framework for corporate governance. The new Corporate Governance Code, recently adopted by the National Bank of Georgia, is expected to address some of the governance challenges facing Georgian banks. Given that TBC Bank and BoG are both listed on the London Stock Exchange through ultimate parent companies, they have a much higher level of governance and transparency than many other banks. They can also attract a much wider investor base. However, this comes at the expense of liquidity in the Georgian securities market as key securities are not listed domestically.

Over 2015-17, there was some consolidation in the Georgian banking market. The number of active banks fell from 21 to 16. Six small banks were no longer active or acquired by TBC Bank/BoG. One microfinance organisation received a banking licence.

The consolidation has been driven by two factors. The National Bank of Georgia (NBG) has introduced stricter regulation and supervision. For example, in 2018 as a result of transitioning to the Basel III framework the NBG introduced increased minimum capital requirements. Market competition (economies of scale and efficiency) is another factor influencing consolidation.

Table A A.1. Consolidation in the Georgian banking market

Timing	Consolidation event
January 2015	Merger of TBC and Bank Constanta
May 2015	Merger of BoG and Privatbank
2016	Progress Bank cancelled its banking licence to become a non-bank institution
September 2016	NBG revoked licence of Caucasus Development Bank; bankruptcy of mother company in Azerbaijan
November 2016	Closure of Capital Bank due to breach of NBG regulations (money laundering)
March 2017	Banking licence for Credo (microfinance)
May 2017	Merger of TBC and Bank Republic

Source: (GET Georgia, 2018[3]).

There is also a high level of foreign capital (15 of 16 banks), with 80% of assets under foreign ownership (through portfolio rather than strategic investors). Georgia is unusual among countries in the region in that it has no state-owned banks. International experience suggests that even highly concentrated banking systems can be efficient and provide access to credit for SMEs.

Trends in the banking sector

There has been strong progress in developing financial intermediation.

Sector performance

In terms of capital, overall Georgian banks are well capitalised. All banks comfortably meet the minimum capital adequacy ratio of 10.5%. Since transition to Basel III in 2018, requirements have changed and they are now different for each bank. The National Bank uses demanding risk weights for foreign currency loans. BoG and TBC Bank have additional buffers. These currency buffers should be maintained given external risks and other vulnerabilities.

Figure A A.2. Regulatory capital adequacy ratio for Georgian banks (Basel III), percentage, 2014-18

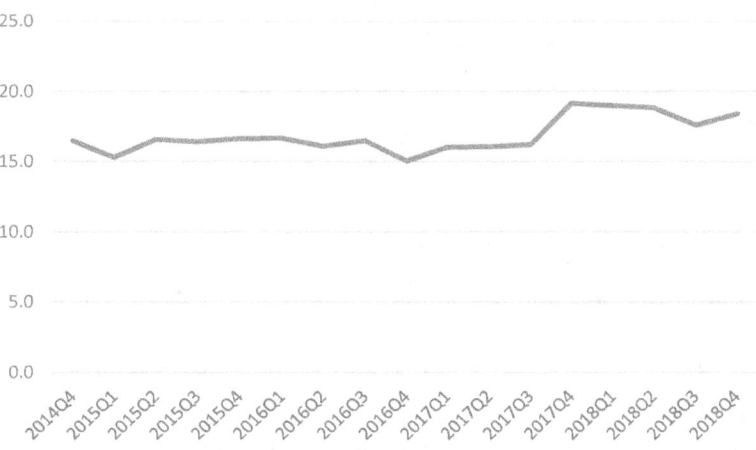

Source: (NBG, 2019[1]).

In terms of asset quality, there has been a long-term decline in the levels of non-performing loans (NPLs) (based on the NBG definition). NPLs declined from 9.5% in early 2013 to 5.5% by the end of 2018. Banks generally employ strong provisioning policies, with active efforts to restructure companies in debt, supported by a new bankruptcy law. There was no major increase in NPLs following depreciation of the Georgian Lari (GEL) in 2015. Due to the rapid growth in retail credit and foreign exchange borrowing, NPLs may increase. However, the National Bank employs strong oversight.

Figure A A.3. Non-performing loans for Georgian banks, share, 2008-18

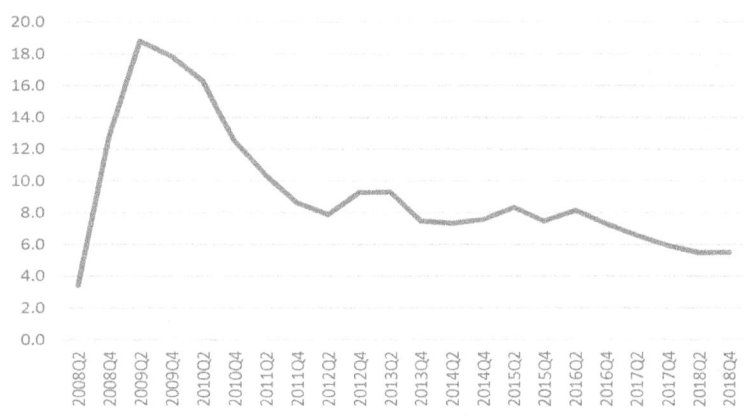

Source: (NBG, 2019[1]).

Profitability across the sector turned negative during the financial crisis, but soon recovered. Return on equity (RoE) in the banking sector is high in Georgia (23.3% in 2018), and much higher than in other banks in the region. A high RoE supports stability in the banking sector, and can be partly explained by good banking efficiency and low impairment charges (e.g. NPLs and default rates).

Figure A A.4. Return on equity of Georgian Banks, 2008-18, share

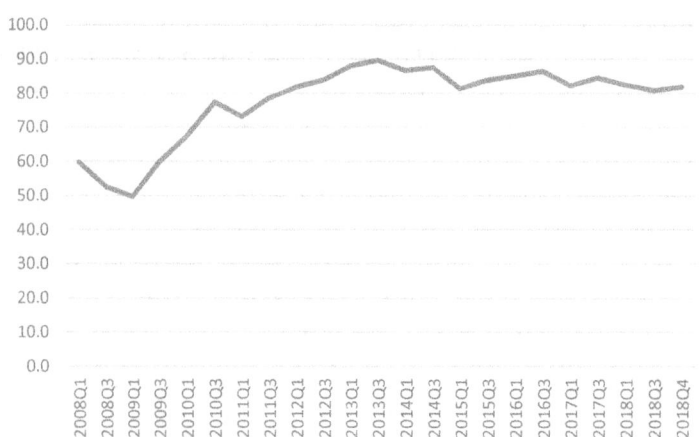

Source: (NBG, 2019[1]).

Georgia's banks enjoy stable funding with increasing deposits since 2014 despite regional tensions and depreciation of the Georgian Lari. There is limited wholesale funding (partly from IFIs). There is a high share of liquid assets, with deposit-to-loan ratios of about 100% at all key banks. There is a high degree of trust among depositors in the banks and the supervisor, and the absence of a deposit insurance scheme has not to date been a problem. Banks generally use conservative funding models. Approximately 38% of deposits are in local currency, with 62% in foreign currency.

Figure A A.5. Georgian banks customer deposits to overall loans, share, 2008-18

Source: (NBG, 2019[1]).

Dollarisation can create risks for banking solvency and financial stability. It can also constrain macro policy (creating a fear of floating currency). On the one hand, lack of a credible monetary regime and high variability in foreign exchange and inflation are key drivers of dollarisation. On the other, inflation targeting and credibility can reduce it. There was a significant decline in loan dollarisation in 2017, helped by the prohibition of foreign currency loans under GEL 100 000. Deposit dollarisation has also been reduced. However, foreign currency is still regarded as a stronger store of value.

Figure A A.6. Share of foreign currency-denominated loans issued by Georgian banks, 2008-18

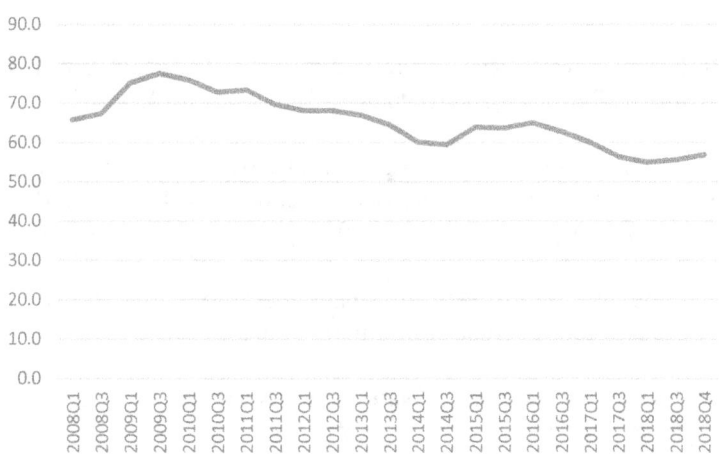

Source: (NBG, 2019[1]).

Ongoing reform

Dollarisation remains the key vulnerability of Georgia's financial system. The preconditions for addressing this are in place. Higher capital requirements for loans denominated in foreign currencies will act as a buffer and reduce risks. The introduction of inflation-indexed bonds would also support this, as well as the development of local-currency long-term debt instruments. There have also been concerns about the close relationship between the banking sector and other areas of the economy. Commercial banking groups have historically had interests across a range of other sectors, including construction, healthcare, tourism, education and winemaking. There have been concerns that banks provide preferable treatment to connected companies. This distorts the market and reduces availability of credit to other businesses (Khundadze, 2017[4]). The National Bank of Georgia and the government introduced regulations to address cross ownership in 2014. However, concerns remain, and the situation requires ongoing monitoring.

Georgia has rather underdeveloped bond and equity markets. Larger companies lack long-dated local-currency debt instruments and risk-oriented capital. Central Europe has demonstrated that both markets can become liquid, even in a small economy. The emergence of Georgia's pension funds and the growing interest of foreign institutional investors would be supportive. Regulatory priorities are to increase concentration of liquidity, enhance transparency at issuance and listing of companies which will help contain self-dealing and/or insider dealing.

Under its Deep and Comprehensive Free Trade Area with the European Union (EU), Georgia has committed to adopt the entire EU financial framework as it evolves. This is in the country's own interest, as it imports a credible legal regime that is well-recognised internationally. But EU rules need to be adapted to the local context. The deposit insurance fund is a good illustration of reflecting much smaller local thresholds. As in all emerging markets, a framework for orderly bank resolution is essential. However, mobilising a potential "bail-in" will depend on establishing credible domestic supervision. Many capital market instruments are not yet developed. Present EU rules could overburden the supervisor unnecessarily and discourage further market development.

References

Agenda.GE (2017), "International finance corporation invests in Bank of Georgia landmark eurobond", *G.E. Agenda,* 2 June, http://agenda.ge/en/news/2017/1099. [2]

GET Georgia (2018), "Banking sector monitoring Georgia 2018", *Policy Study Series*, No. PS/01, German Economic Team Georgia/Berlin Economics, Tibilisi/Berlin, https://www.get-georgia.de/wp-content/uploads/2018/03/PS_01_2018_en.pdf. [3]

Khundadze, T. (2017), "The two faces of Georgia's banking sector", *OC Media,* 31 March, http://oc-media.org/the-two-faces-of-georgias-banking-sector/. [4]

NBG (2019), *Financial Soundness Indicators*, National Bank of Georgia, webpage (accessed 23 October 2019), https://www.nbg.gov.ge/index.php?m=304. [1]

Annex B. SME low-cost energy and resource efficiency investments

Name of RECP investment measure	Brief project description including expected environmental benefits and cost savings	Total investment cost, EUR	Company type
Improved energy efficiency at an asphalt producing factory	• Recovering the heat of exhaust gases coming out of the outlet of the heat exchanging tube for heating the bitumen tank and bitumen internal part. Installation of exhaust gas collectors for the heat recovery • Using special hydro-insulating cover which must be placed on piles of inert materials when raining or snowing • Installing heat insulation of the bitumen pipeline • Improved energy efficiency will reduce emissions of CO_2 and other pollutants into the atmosphere and will also improve environment quality at the factory site. • Annual CO_2 emission reduction: 82.9 tonnes; cost savings: EUR 13 503	6 300	Small-sized asphalt producing company, 38 employees
Reduction of natural gas and bitumen consumption for drying the inert material and mineral powder; installation of additional equipment	• Covering the inert materials stored in open air with a special waterproof material (2 000 m²) and arranging water drainage channels of up to 200 m. As a result of this measure, 37 500 m³ of natural gas or EUR 10 240 per year will be saved • Roofing one section of the open type bitumen reservoir including metal construction, channel # 10, square pipe 60 * 100mm and roofing sheet 0.5mm. This measure will lead to saving up to 4 000m³ of natural gas per year, equivalent to EUR 1 100 • Using a Surface Active Agents technology will save up to 32 tonnes of bitumen per year. To install this technology special equipment is needed and direct contact with the producers of these substances. This technology results in cost savings of EUR 11 076 per year	9 450	Medium-sized road construction company, 135 employees
Reducing energy consumption of equipment installed in an artisanal way: heat insulation and solar collectors	• Installing heat insulation using a new mine well cap equipment • Installing 6 south-oriented units of vacuum 30-tube solar collector to reduce electricity consumption, the solar installation will generate heat in winter time, while during the summer it will heat water without using electricity Estimates show that changing the mine well cap construction and arranging additional thermal insulation will result in electricity consumption of 10 275 kWh, which is equivalent to 10% of the energy currently consumed by the company, this in turn translates into EUR 780 of annual savings. As a result of the installation of the vacuum 30-tube solar collectors for water heating, electricity savings will reach 32 900 kWh, which is equivalent to 75% of the energy currently consumed, this will enabling the company to save EUR 1 900 per year	6 200	Medium-sized metalware production company, 41 employees
Substituting the fossil fuel used for steam generation with relatively cheaper energy source – biofuel	• Grape ridge from wine making will be used as a biofuel, significant amounts of grape ridge are stored in local wineries. Malt husk can also be used as bio fuel for heat generation • The proposed heat generator can be assembled in the local metal construction factory • Replacing the boiler operating on natural gas with a heat generator operating on biofuel will increase the production efficiency of the company by reducing the cost of heat generation. This measure will also reduce waste generated in the production process of wineries in the region	15 000	Small-sized brewery, 38 employees

Name of RECP investment measure	Brief project description including expected environmental benefits and cost savings	Total investment cost, EUR	Company type
Substituting the fossil fuel used for steam generation with a relatively cheaper biofuel: replacing a boiler operating on natural gas	• Replacing the boiler operating on natural gas with a heat generator operating on biofuel. In this case, 10 tonnes of biofuel (grape ridge) will be consumed instead of 5 578 m³ of natural gas. Annually, this will result in 130-140 tonnes of grape ridge used (remaining as waste from wine making) with energy potential estimated at the equivalent of 75-80 000 m³ of natural gas. In addition, 11 tonnes of CO_2 emissions can annually be reduced • Despite a small NPV for a 5-year project, the project will have a considerable environmental impact as it will help introducing a Circular Economy approach at the enterprise	5 500	Small-sized wine and cognac producing enterprise, 55 employees

Note: As part of the EU-funded EaP GREEN project, UNIDO's work on Resource Efficient and Cleaner Production (RECP) in the manufacturing sector in Georgia was focused on supporting SMEs to identify RECP measures and prepare projects to finance them. The projects included in this table come from UNIDO's work on the ground. The examples show the potential environmental and cost savings that small businesses can achieve as a result of implementing RECP measures. The examples also show that many of these typical energy and resource efficiency investments by small firms are low-cost measures and fall in this middle segment of green investments, which are not interesting either for microfinance organisations or for traditional banks. This gap in the market of environmental finance for SMEs needs government attention.
Source: Information provided by UNIDO.